The
Classic Guide
to
BREADMAKING

The
Classic Guide
to
BREADMAKING

Sylvester Graham &
Robert Wells

AMBERLEY

First published by Light & Stearns in 1837 W. H. Allen & Co. in 1875
This edition by Amberley Publishing, 2016

Amberley Publishing
The Hill, Stroud
Gloucestershire, GL5 4EP

www.amberley-books.com

Copyright © Amberley Publishing, 2016

British Library Cataloguing in Publication Data.
A catalogue record for this book is available from the British Library.

ISBN 978 1 4456 5209 2 (print)
ISBN 978 1 4456 5210 8 (ebook)

Typesetting and Origination by Amberley Publishing.
Printed in the UK.

Contents

Editor's Note   7

Preface   9

A Treatise on Bread   11

Preface   13

History of Bread   15

Laws of Diet   21

Material of Bread   29

Properties of Bread   41

Fermentation   55

Preparation of Bread   65

Who Should Make Bread   75

Varieties of Bread   91

The Modern Practical Bread Baker   105

Preface   107

Flour   109

On Yeasts and Barms   115

Fermentation   131

Sponging   139

The Manipulation of Dough   155

Brown Bread, Wheat meal, Rye, etc.   177

Substitutes for Wheat Bread   185

Ovens   191

General Details   199

Machinery, Tools, etc.   205

Adulteration   213

Appendix   221

Editor's Note

This book contains texts by Sylvester Graham and Robert Wells, published in 1837 and 1875 respectively. The original language has been retained as it appeared in these editions, and this displays both authors' personal styles, but also a very different way of thinking from the modern day on a variety of topics. At times, views expressed in the text may appear rather surprising, but it is important to remember that at the time of writing certain (no-longer held) views prevailed. This volume nevertheless offers the reader an important historical insight into a fascinating pastime and trade.

Preface

Popular around the world, bread takes many different forms depending on where in the world you walk into a bakery. In India, flat breads such as chapatti are king, whereas in Sweden you're more likely to be treated to some knäckebröd – a rye-based 'crispbread'.

A staple of our diet, from the lowliest table to the dining rooms of the upper crust, bread has enriched our lives for thousands of years – in Britain alone, the history of bread stretches back to 3700 BC. Dating back to 1837 and 1875, the two texts contained in this volume offer a fascinating glimpse into the world of breadmaking in the nineteenth century and how attitudes developed over the course of fifty years that followed the industrial revolution.

The first text, penned by American dietary reformer Sylvester Graham, extols the virtues of making bread in your own home. Originally published as *A Treatise on Bread* by Light & Stearns of Boston, he gives an eighteenth-century history of bread, what he describes as the 'laws of diet' and the ingredients and methods needed to bake the perfect loaf. He also looks at the fermentation process and the variety of bread the average American could produce in the comfort of their own kitchen.

In the second text included here, Robert Wells' *The Modern Practical Baker*, the author takes a different tact. Nearly forty years had passed since Sylvester Graham encouraged American homesteads to rise up and bake their own, but Wells attempted to slice the issue another way. Looking to separate the wheat from the chaff, he instead encourages a more mechanised, industrial approach to breadmaking, and the benefits of baking on a larger scale. A doughty businessman, Wells sought to promote the artisanal value of breadmaking, and the value of professional bakeries. Whereas Graham appealed to the individual, Wells' work was instead aimed at the trade and those who worked within the industry.

Printed here in the same volume for the first time, *The Classic Guide to Breadmaking* combines these two works to offer a compelling look at two very different approaches to bread. These fascinating time capsules still feel relevant today, as supermarkets continue to market their own large-scale freshly baked bread while a growing number of hobbyists, encouraged by an increasing array of television shows and celebrity bakers, instead choose to bake in their comfort of their home.

But whether you prefer buying or baking, a dependable white loaf or a hearty sourdough, it is hard to imagine bread disappearing from the menu anytime in the near future. So, let's raise a toast: to bread.

The Editor

A Treatise on Bread

Sylvester Graham

Preface

There are probably few people in civilized life, who – were the question put to them directly – would not say, that they consider bread one of the most, if not the most important article of diet which enters into the food of man. And yet there is, in reality, almost a total and universal carelessness about the character of bread. Thousands in civic life will, for years, and perhaps as long as they live, eat the most miserable trash that can be imagined, in the form of bread, and never seem to think that they can possibly have anything better, nor even that it is an evil to eat such vile stuff as they do. And if there is occasionally an individual who is troubled with some convictions that his bread is not quite what it should be, he knows not how to remedy the difficulty; for it is a serious truth, that, although nearly every human being in civilized life eats bread of some kind or other, yet scarcely any one has sufficient knowledge of the true principles and processes concerned in bread-making, and of the actual causes of the bad qualities of bread, to know how, with any degree of certainty, to avoid bad and secure good bread.

I have thought, therefore, that I could hardly do society a better service, than to publish the following treatise on a subject which, whether people are aware of it or not, is, in reality, of very great importance to the health and comfort of every one.

It has been prepared for the press with more haste, under more embarrassments from other engagements, and with less severity of revision, than I could wish. Yet, whatever may be its defects of arrangement, method or style, I have taken care to have the principles correct, and the instructions such as, if attended to, will enable every one who is heartily devoted to the object, to make good bread.

I must, however, acknowledge, that I have very little expectation that proper attention will be paid to this subject, so long as the dietetic habits of society continue to be what they are. While the various preparations of animal food constitute so important a portion of human aliment, the quality of bread will be greatly disregarded and neglected, and people will continue almost universally to be cursed with poor bread.

Nevertheless, I trust some good will be done by the little work I now send out; and I am not without hope, that it will be the means of a considerable improvement in the quality of bread, and, as a natural and necessary consequence, an improvement in the health and happiness of those who consume it.

That it may prove thus beneficial to my fellow creatures in a high degree, is my hearty and fervent desire.

S. GRAHAM.
Northampton, April 12, 1837.

History of Bread

Primitive food of man. Bruising and grinding grain. Baking.
Invention of leavened bread. Bread among the Greeks and
Romans – among the Hebrews. Simplicity of the bread now
used in many countries.

In the English version of the sacred scriptures, the term Bread
is frequently used to signify vegetable food in general. Thus in
Gen. iii, 19, the Lord says to Adam – 'In the sweat of thy face
shalt thou eat bread (or food) till thou return to the ground.'
See also Gen. xviii, 5, and xxviii, 20, and Ex. ii, 20.

The most extended sense of the word, however, according
to general usage, comprehends all farinaceous vegetable
substances which enter into the diet of man; such as the
farinaceous seeds or grain, nuts, fruit, roots, &c. And in this
extended sense, Bread, in some form or other, has been the
principal article in the diet of mankind, from the earliest
generations of the human race, to the present time; except
among the few small and scattered tribes, which have, perhaps,
ever since the days of Noah, in different parts of the earth,
subsisted mainly on animal food.

It is nearly certain that the primitive inhabitants of the earth
ate their food with very little, if any artificial preparation.

The various fruits, nuts, seeds, roots, and other vegetable substances on which they fed, were eaten by them in their natural state, with no other grinding than that which was done by the teeth.

As the human family increased, and population became more dense and extended, and providential measures more necessary, the condition and circumstances of society gradually led to the invention and adoption of the simple, and, at first, rude arts of domestic life. Among these, was that of bruising the harder articles of their food, such as nuts and seeds, or grain, on flat stones, selected and kept for the purpose. By constant use, these stones in time became hollowed out; and being thereby rendered more convenient, men at length began to form mortars and pestles from stones; and probably the next step was the construction of the rude kind of hand-mills, which continued in use for many centuries; and indeed, which, with the stone mortars, have, throughout all ages and in almost every portion of the earth, been used in the ruder states of society.

When men became acquainted with the use of fire, they probably often parched their com or grain before they pounded it; and afterwards, they learned to mix it with water into the consistency of dough, and to bake this, in an unleavened or unfermented state, on flat stones before the fire, or in the hot ashes or hot earth, or in the rude ovens which they formed by digging holes in the earth, into which they put heated stones, and slightly covered them with leaves or grass, and then laid in the article they wished to bake, and over this strewed some leaves, and then covered the whole with earth. (In this same manner the Sandwich Islanders cooked all their food, when they were first discovered.)

This kind of unleavened bread undoubtedly constituted a very important, if not the principal article of artificially prepared food in the diet of the primitive inhabitants of the earth, for many centuries; and the same, or very nearly the same kind of bread continued in general use down to the days of Abraham; and it is probable that the unleavened bread used by his descendants at the feast of the Passover, before and after they left Egypt, was of the same kind.

It is hardly possible, however, that it could have been otherwise, than that, at a much earlier period, larger quantities of this dough were occasionally made, than were immediately baked, and consequently portions of it were suffered to stand and ferment; and by this means, men in process of time learned to make leavened, or raised bread.

At how early a date loaf or raised bread came into common use, it is impossible now to ascertain with any considerable degree of precision. The scriptures do not afford us any evidence that Abraham was accustomed to such bread; but the fact that Moses, at the institution of the supper of the Passover, the night before the Jews left Egypt, commanded them strictly to abstain from leavened bread, and to eat only the unleavened, proves conclusively that the Israelites at least, were then accustomed to fermented, or raised bread.

Neither history nor tradition enables us to speak with any degree of confidence in regard to the period at which other nations became acquainted with the art of bread-making; but from all that has come down to us from ancient times, we learn that the primitive generations of every nation subsisted on fruits and other products of the vegetable kingdom, in their uncooked or natural state.

The Greeks assert that they were taught the art of making bread by their god, Pan; and Pliny informs us that this art was not known at Rome till near six hundred years after the foundation of that city. The Roman armies, he says, on their return from Macedonia, brought Grecian bakers into Italy. Before this time, the Romans prepared their meal in a kind of pap or soft pudding; and on this account Pliny calls them pap eaters.

But though the Egyptians and Israelites were probably among the earliest portions of the human family who became acquainted with the art of making loaf or raised bread, the quality of their bread continued to be exceedingly simple and coarse for many generations.

Even after the establishment of the Hebrew nation in Palestine – in the most splendid days of Jerusalem – at the period of the highest refinement of the Jews, in the arts of civil and domestic life, their fine flour, from which their choicest bread and cakes were made, was, in comparison with modern superfine flour, extremely coarse – ground mostly by females, in hand-mills constructed and kept for that purpose.

From Rome the art of bread-making very slowly found its way over considerable portions of Europe. A thousand years after Julius Caesar first entered Britain, the rude people of that country were little acquainted with raised bread. 'Even at present,' says Prof. Thomson, 'loaf bread is seldom used except by the higher classes of inhabitants, in the northern countries of Europe and Asia.'

In Eastern and Southern Asia, rice constitutes the principal bread-stuff; and this is generally prepared with great simplicity. In Middle and Western Asia, and in Africa, bread, though made of different kinds of grain, is prepared with almost equal simplicity. In Scotland, Ireland, and indeed throughout Europe generally, barley, oats, rye, potatoes, peas, beans, chestnuts, and other farinaceous vegetables, constitute the bread-stuff of most of the laboring people, or peasantry. In the islands of the Pacific and Southern oceans, the bread of the inhabitants consists of the plantain, bananas, yams, bread-fruit, and other like vegetables, simply roasted, baked, or boiled.

Bread, therefore, of some kind or other, made of some of the farinaceous products of the vegetable kingdom, has probably, in almost every portion of the world, and every period of time, been one of the first, and most important, and universal articles of food, artificially prepared by cooking, which has entered into the diet of mankind; and hence it has with great propriety been called 'the staff of life.'

Laws of Diet

Reasons why food in its natural state would be the best. Concentrated nutriment. Interesting experiments on animals. Mixtures of food. Leavened and unleavened bread. Qualifications of the best bread.

If man were to subsist wholly on alimentary substances in their natural state, or without any artificial preparation by cooking, then he would be obliged to use his teeth freely in masticating his food; and by so doing, not only preserve his teeth from decay, and keep them in sound health, but at the same time, and by the same means, would he thoroughly mix his food with the fluid of his mouth, and thus prepare it both for swallowing and for the action of the stomach, and by the same means also, he would be made to swallow his food slowly, as the welfare of the stomach and of the whole system requires he should.

Again, if man were to subsist wholly on uncooked food, he would never suffer from the improper temperature of his aliment. Hot substances taken into the mouth serve more directly and powerfully to destroy the teeth than any other cause which acts immediately upon them; and hot food and drink received into the stomach always in some degree debilitate that organ, and through it, every other organ and portion of the whole system; diminishing, as an ultimate result, the vital power of every part – impairing every function, and increasing the susceptibility of the whole body to the action of disturbing causes, and predisposing it to disease. Again, if man were to subsist entirely on food in a natural state, he would never suffer from concentrated aliment. Every substance in nature which God has prepared for the food of man consists of both nutritious and innutritious matter. The proportions vary in different kinds of food. Thus in a hundred pounds of potatoes, there are about twenty-five pounds of nourishing matter; while in a hundred pounds of good wheat there are about eighty pounds of nourishing matter. There are a few products of the vegetable kingdom which are still higher in the scale of nutriment, than wheat; and on the other hand there is a boundless variety ranging below wheat, extending down to three or four per cent of nourishment. But nature, without the aid of human art, produces nothing for the alimentary use of man which is purely a concentrated nutrient substance. And God has constructed man in strict accordance with this general economy of nature. He has organized and endowed the human body with reference to the condition and qualities of those substances in nature which He designed for the food of man. And consequently, while man obeys the laws of constitution and relation which should govern him in regard to his food, he preserves the health and integrity of his alimentary organs, and through them of his whole nature; and so far as his dietetic habits are concerned, secures the highest and best condition of his nature. But, if he disregards these laws, and by artificial means greatly departs from the natural adaptation of things, he inevitably brings evil on himself and on his posterity.

It has been fully proved that 'bulk, or a due proportion of innutritious matter in our food, is quite as important to health as nourishment.' Human beings may subsist from childhood to extreme old age on good potatoes and pure water alone, and enjoy the best and most uninterrupted health, and possess the greatest muscular power and ability to endure protracted fatigue and exposure. But if the purely nutrient matter of the potato be separated out by artificial means, and human beings, fed exclusively on this concentrated form of aliment and pure water, they will soon perish, because the alimentary organs of man are not constituted and endowed for such kinds of food. And this is true of all animals, in the higher orders at least.

We know that dogs fed on sugar and water, gum and water, fine flour bread and water, or any other kind of concentrated aliment, will soon languish, and droop, and emaciate, and die; but if a due proportion of proper innutritious substance be mixed with these concentrated forms of aliment, the dogs will subsist on them and remain healthy. So if horses, cows, deer, sheep, and other grass-eating animals be fed on grain alone, they will soon lose their appetite and begin to droop, and will shortly perish; but if a due proportion of straw or shavings of wood be given them with their grain, they will continue to do well. Man is affected in the same manner. He cannot long subsist on purely nutritious substances. And the reason is not because these substances have no azote or nitrogen in them; nor is it because man *necessarily* requires a variety of alimentary substances, but simply and exclusively because the anatomical construction and vital powers of the alimentary organs are constitutionally adapted to alimentary substances which consist of both nutritious and innutritious matter; and therefore a due proportion of innutritious matter in the food of man is as essential to the welfare of his alimentary organs, as a due proportion of nourishment is to the support of his body.

Again, if man subsisted wholly on uncooked food, he would not only be preserved from improper concentrations, but also from pernicious combinations of alimentary substances. The alimentary organs of man, like those of the horse, ox, sheep, dog, cat, and most or all other animals of the higher orders, if not in fact, of all other animals without limitation, possess the vital capability of so accommodating themselves to emergencies, that they can be made to digest almost every vegetable and animal substance in nature; and they can, by long training, be educated to digest a mixture of these substances at the same time. Nevertheless it is incontestibly true, that the alimentary organs of man and of all other animals, can manage one kind of food at a time better than a mixed ingestion; for it is impossible that the solvent fluids secreted by the stomach and other organs belonging to the alimentary apparatus, should be at the same time equally well adapted to entirely different kinds of food.

I do not say that the alimentary organs of man cannot, by long habit, be brought into such a condition as that, while that condition remains, they will not manage a mixed ingestion of animal and vegetable food, with more immediate comfort and satisfaction to themselves and the individual, than they will an ingestion of pure vegetable food. But this does not militate against the general principle in the least; for it is nevertheless true, that the same organs are capable of being brought into a condition in which they will manage an ingestion of unmixed food of either kind, with less embarrassment and injury to themselves and the whole system, than they can the mixed food in any condition. Hence it is a general law of nature, concerning the dietetic habits of man, that simplicity of food at each meal is essential to the highest well-being of the individual and of the race.

God has unquestionably provided a great and rich variety of substances for man's nourishment and enjoyment; but it is equally certain that he did not design that man should partake of all this variety at a single meal, nor in a single day, nor season – but from meal to meal, from day to day, and from season to season, varying his enjoyment in strictest consistency with the great laws of his nature. And hence all artificial combinations of alimentary substances, and particularly those of a heterogeneous kind, and yet more especially the concentrated forms, must be more or less pernicious to the alimentary organs, and through them to the whole system.

Finally, if man subsisted wholly on uncooked food, the undepraved integrity of his appetite, his thorough mastication and slow swallowing, and his simple meal, would greatly serve to prevent his overeating, and thus save him from the ruinous effects of one of the most destructive causes operating in civic life.

Whatever may be the material, therefore, from which bread is made, when the artificial preparation is of that simple character which leaves the proportions of nutritious and innutritious properties, as nature combined them, and effects little change in the nutritious principles, and retains the natural requisition for the function of the teeth, and thus secures the proper chewing of the food and the mixing of it with the fluids of the mouth, and swallowing of it slowly, the artificial process militates very little, if at all, against any of the physiological or vital interests of the body. But if our artificial process of bread-making, concentrates the nutrient properties, and destroys the due proportion between the bulk and nourishment, and forms improper changes and combinations in the nutrient elements, and does away the necessity for mastication or chewing, and presents the food in too elevated a temperature, or too hot, and enables us to swallow it too rapidly, with little or no exercise of the teeth, and without properly mixing it with the fluids of the mouth, the artificial process of cooking is decidedly and often exceedingly inimical, not only to the vital interests of the alimentary organs, but of the whole human system.

In all civilized nations, and particularly in civic life, bread, as I have already stated, is by far the most important article of food which is artificially prepared; and in our country and climate, it is the most important article that enters into the diet of man; and therefore it is of the first consideration, that its character should, in every respect, be as nearly as possible consistent with the laws of constitution and relation established in our nature; or with the anatomical construction and vital properties and powers and interest of our systems.

If we contemplate the human constitution in its highest and best condition – in the possession of its most vigorous and unimpaired powers – and ask, what must be the character of our bread in order to preserve that constitution in that condition? the answer most indubitably is that the coarse unleavened bread of early times, when of proper age, was one of the least removes from the natural state of food – one of the simplest and most wholesome forms of artificial preparations, and best adapted to fulfil the laws of constitution and relation; and therefore best adapted to sustain the most vigorous and healthy state of the alimentary organs, and the highest and best condition of the whole nature of man, as a general and permanent fact; and hence it is very questionable whether loaf or raised bread can be made equally conducive to all the interests of our nature, with the simple unleavened bread.

I am aware that many professional men entertain a very different opinion on this subject, and speak of unleavened bread as being less nourishing and less easily digested. This may be true to a limited extent, in special cases of impaired and debilitated alimentary organs; but I am confident that as a general fact the notion is entirely erroneous.

'The whole people of Asia,' says Dr. Cullen, 'live upon unfermented rice. The Americans, before they became acquainted with the Europeans, employed, and for the most part, still employ their maize in the same condition. Even in Europe, the employment of unfermented bread, and unfermented farinaceae in other forms, is still very considerable, and we are ready to maintain that the morbid consequences of such a diet are very seldom to be observed. In Scotland, nine tenths of the lower classes of people – and that is the greater part of the whole – live upon unfermented bread and unfermented farinaceae in other forms, and at the same time, I am of opinion that there are not a more healthy people anywhere to be found. We give it to all classes and both sexes with advantage.'

It is incontestibly true, that if two portions of the same kind of wheat meal be taken and made, the one into unleavened and the other into leavened bread, and both be eaten warm from the oven, the leavened bread will prove much more oppressive and difficult to manage in the stomach than the unleavened. But aside from the changes that are produced by the process of fermentation, there are many other considerations why unleavened bread of a proper quality and age, is better adapted to sustain the alimentary organs and general constitution of man, in their highest and best condition.

Nevertheless, it is very certain, that loaf or raised bread can be made so nearly in accordance with the vital laws and interests of our bodies, as scarcely to militate against them in any perceptible or appreciable degree. And when I say this, I mean not merely its effects on the health and longevity of a single individual, but its effects upon the human constitution, through successive generations, for a thousand years or more.

As a general criterion or rule, then, in regard to the character of bread, we perceive that the most perfect loaf or raised bread, is that which, being made of the best material, is light, and sweet, and well baked, and still most nearly retains all the natural proportions and properties of the original material.

Material of Bread

Wheat. Extent of climate favorable to it. Injured by improper tillage. Removal of impurities. Washing of grain. Separation of the bran from the nutrient particles improper. Ancient Roman bread. Public bakers. Use of bad flour. Adulterations. Poisonous agents used to disguise them.

Among the materials used for making bread in our country – and, in fact, of all the known productions of the vegetable kingdom in any country, wheat is decidedly the best; and it is a remarkable fact, that wheat comes nearer to man than perhaps any other plant, in its power of becoming adapted to different climates, over a wide extent of the earth's surface, so that it may almost be said that wherever the human species can flourish, there wheat can be cultivated.

'It is not certainly known,' says Prof. Thomson, 'in what country wheat was first produced. Mr Bruce informs us that he found it growing wild in Abyssinia; and in his opinion, that kingdom is the native country of the plant. It would seem,' continues the Professor, 'to be originally an African plant, since it thrives best in Barbary and Egypt; and perhaps the mountains of Abyssinia, though within the torrid zone, may not differ much in point of climate, from the more northern plains of Egypt. Wheat is perhaps cultivated over a greater extent of the globe than any other plant. Excellent crops are raised as far north as Sweden, in latitude 60°; it is cultivated in the East Indies, considerably within the limits of the torrid zone; and in the North of Hindostan, it constitutes a chief article in the food of the inhabitants. In India, however, the plant seems to have deteriorated. It is always dwarfish, and the crop is said to be less abundant than in more northern climates.' Yet a cold climate is not most genial to the nature of this plant. 'The wheat of France is superior to that of England; the wheat of Italy is still better than that of France; and perhaps the best of all is raised in Barbary and Egypt.'

Excellent wheat is raised in the southern, and western, and middle portions of the United States; and even in the northern and eastern parts of New England, very fine crops have been produced.

But the wheat and other cultivated products of the vegetable kingdom appropriated to the nourishment of man, like those on which our domestic animals subsist, are too generally, in civilized life, very considerably deteriorated, as to their wholesomeness, by the improper tillage of the soil. I have no doubt that it is true, as stated by those who have made the experiment, that the flour of wheat raised on a cultivated soil recently dressed with crude, stable manure, may readily be distinguished by its odor, from the flour of wheat raised on a new and undepraved soil, or from that raised on a cultivated soil which has been dressed with properly digested manure. And if such and similar results of improper tillage can become the sources of serious evil to the human family, through their effects on the flesh of animals which man devours, and on the milk and butter which he consumes, surely the immediate effects of such a deteriorated vegetable aliment on the human system, must be very considerable.

They who have never eaten bread made of wheat, recently produced by a pure virgin soil, have but a very imperfect notion of the deliciousness of good bread; such as is often to be met with in the comfortable log houses in our western country. It is probably true that the new soil, in its virgin purity, before it becomes exhausted by tillage, and debauched by the means which man uses to enrich and stimulate it, produces most, if not all kinds of vegetables appropriate for human aliment, in a more perfect and healthy state, than any soil which has been long under cultivation, can be made to do. Nevertheless, by a proper application of physiological principles to agriculture, many of the evils which now result from improper tillage may easily be avoided, and the quality of all those vegetable substances which enter into the diet of man may be very greatly improved, both in regard to wholesomeness and deliciousness.

But while the people of our country are so entirely given up as they are at present, to gross and promiscuous feeding on the dead carcasses of animals, and to the untiring pursuits of wealth, it is perhaps wholly in vain for a single individual to raise his voice on a subject of this kind. The farmer will continue to be most eager to increase the number of his acres, and to extort from those acres the greatest amount of produce, with the least expense of tillage, and with little or no regard to the quality of that produce in relation to the physiological interests of man; while the people generally, are contented to gratify their depraved appetites on whatever comes before them, without pausing to inquire whether their indulgences are adapted to preserve or to destroy their health and life. Yet if some one does not raise a voice upon this subject which shall be heard and heeded, there will soon reach us, as a nation, a voice of calamity which we shall not be able to shut our ears against, albeit we may in the perverseness of our sensualism, incorrigibly persist in disregarding its admonitions, till the deep chastisements of outraged nature shall reach the very 'bone and marrow' of the human constitution, and fill our land with such a living rottenness, as now in some other portions of the earth, renders human society odious and abominable.

Whether, therefore, my voice shall be heard and heeded or not, I will obey the dictates of my sense of duty, and solemnly declare that this subject demands the prompt and earnest attention of every agriculturist and of every friend to the common cause of humanity; for it is most certain, that until the agriculture of our country is conducted in strict accordance with physiological truth, it is not possible for us to realize those physical, and intellectual, and moral, and social, and civil blessings for which the human constitution and our soil and climate are naturally capacitated.

When proper attention has been paid to the character of the wheat itself, the next thing is to see that it is thoroughly cleansed.

Sometimes, in consequence of the peculiarities of the season, or climate, or soil, or some other cause, there will be a species of disease affecting the wheat and other grains; and this may be of such a character as not easily to be removed nor counteracted by any means; but more generally the rust, and smut, and dust, which attach themselves to the skin of the grain, may, by proper care, be so far removed, as at least to render the meal or flour far more pure and wholesome than it otherwise would be. And here let me remark, that they are greatly deceived, who suppose that the bolting cloth which separates the fine flour from the outer skin or bran, also separates the impurities attached to the outer skin from the flour. By the process of grinding, these impurities are rubbed from the outer skin, and made quite as fine as any portion of the flour, and for the most part pass with the fine flour through the bolting cloth.

To remedy this, it is perhaps generally true, that in large flouring establishments, a kind of smut or scouring mill is in operation, through which the wheat passes, and is pretty thoroughly rubbed or scoured without being broken; and after this, it passes through a screen or winnowing mill, and thus is tolerably well cleansed and prepared for grinding. Yet this process by no means renders the wheat so perfectly clean and wholesome as washing.

Those who have given little attention to this subject, will probably think that the trouble of washing all their bread stuff before it is ground, would be much greater than any benefit which would result from it. But a short experience in the matter, would convince every one who has a proper regard for the character of his bread, that the trouble of washing his grain bears no comparison to the improvement effected by it. Indeed, they who become accustomed to washing their grain, will soon cease to regard it as a trouble; and the improvement in the whiteness and sweetness of their bread will be so great, that they would be extremely unwilling to relinquish the practice.

When people are so situated that they can have things as they wish, they will also find that their bread is much richer, if the grain is ground but a short time before it is cooked.

The best way, therefore, is, for every family to raise or purchase a sufficient quantity of the best new wheat that can be produced by proper tillage in a good soil, and put that away in clean casks or bins, where it will be kept perfectly dry and sweet; and, according to the size of the family, take, from time to time, as they need it, one or two bushels, and wash it thoroughly but briskly in two or three waters, and then spread it out on a drying sheet or table, made for the purpose, and which is considerably inclined, so that the water remaining with the wheat will easily run off.

The skin or bran of the wheat is so well protected by its own oily property, that little or no water will penetrate it, unless it be suffered to remain in the water much longer than is necessary. Being thinly spread out upon the sheet or table in a good drying day, it will be sufficiently dry in a few hours for grinding. And I say again, let any one who loves good bread, wash his grain a few times in this manner, and he will be very reluctant to return to the use of bread made of unwashed grain.

It would be difficult to ascertain at how early a period in the progress of society, mankind, in the preparation of wheat for bread-making, began to put asunder what God has joined together, and to concentrate the more purely nutrient properties, by separating the flour from the part commonly called the bran. The Bible speaks of fine flour or meal, as a portion of the meat offerings of the temple, but it is not probable this approached very near to the superfine flour of the present time.

We are informed also that the Romans, more than two thousand years ago, had four or five different kinds of bread – one of which was made of the purest flour, from which all the bran was separated. This was eaten only by the rich and luxurious. A second kind, in more common use, was that from which a portion of the bran was taken; and a third kind, which was more generally used than any other, was that which was made of the whole substance of the wheat. A fourth kind was made mostly of the bran, for dogs.

But at whatever period in the history of the race this artificial process was commenced, certain it is that in direct violation of the laws of constitution and relation which the Creator has established in the nature of man, this process of mechanical analysis is, at the present day, carried to the full extent of possibility; and the farina, and gluten, and saccharine matter of the wheat, are almost perfectly concentrated in the form of superfine flour. Nor is this all – these concentrated nutrient properties of the wheat are mixed and complicated in ways innumerable, with other concentrated substances, to pamper the depraved appetites of man, with kinds of food which always and inevitably tend to impair his health and to abbreviate his life.

Even the bread, which is the simplest form into which human ingenuity tortures the flour of wheat, is, by other causes besides the concentration I have named, too frequently rendered the instrument of disease and death, rather than the means of life and health, to those that eat it.

In cities and large towns, most people depend on public bakers for their bread. And I have no doubt that public bakers, as a body, are as honest and worthy a class of men as any in society. I have no wish to speak evil of any one; and it is always painful to me to find myself compelled, in fidelity to the common cause of humanity, to expose the faults of any particular class of men, when probably every other class in society is as deeply involved in errors which, in the sight of God, evince, at least, an equal degree of moral turpitude.

But public bakers, like other men, who serve the public more for the sake of securing their own emolument than for the public good, have always had recourse to various expedients in order to increase the lucrativeness of their business.

To secure custom and profit at the same time, they have considered it necessary that a given quantity of flour should be made into a loaf as large and as white as possible, and free from any disagreeable taste, while at the same time it retains the greatest possible weight.

From a variety of causes, the quality and price of flour have always been very unstable. Sometimes the crops are small, or the foreign demand for flour or the home consumption is unusually great, or the season is unfavorable to the health of grain, and the wheat becomes diseased, or the harvest time is unfavorable, and the wheat sprouts before it is secured, or large quantities of flour become soured or musty, or in some other manner damaged.

To counteract these things, and to make the most profitable use of such flour as the market affords them, the public bakers have been led to try various experiments with chemical agents, and there is reason to believe that in numerous instances, they have been too successful in their practices for the well being of those who have been the consumers of their bread.

According to treatises on breadmaking, which have within a few years past appeared in European scientific journals, 'alum, sulphate of zinc, sub-carbonate of magnesia, sub-carbonate of ammonia, sulphate of copper, and several other substances, have been used by public bakers in making bread; and some of these substances have been employed by them to a very great extent, and with very great success in the cause of their cupidity. They have not only succeeded by such means, in making light and white bread out of extremely poor flour, but they have also been able so to disguise their adulterations, as to work in with their flour, without being detected by the consumers, a portion of the flour of beans, peas and potatoes – and even chalk, pipe clay and plaster of Paris, have been employed to increase the weight and whiteness of their bread.'

'The use of alum in bread-making,' says a distinguished chemist, 'appears to be very ancient. It is one of those articles which have been the most extensively and successfully used in disguising bad flour, and the various adulterations of bread. Its injurious action upon the health is not to be compared with that of sulphate of copper, and yet, daily taken into the stomach, it may seriously affect the system.'

'Thirteen bakers were condemned on the 27th of January, 1829, by the correctional tribunal of Brussels, for mixing sulphate of copper or blue vitriol with their bread. It makes the bread very white, light, large and porous, but rather tasteless; and it also enables the bread to retain a greater quantity of water, and thereby very considerably increases its weight. A much larger quantity of alum is necessary to produce these effects; but when of sufficient quantity, it strengthens the paste, and, as the bakers say, "makes the bread swell large".'

If the statements of our large druggists can be relied on, the public bakers of our own country probably employ ammonia more freely, at present, than any other substance I have named.

Pearlash or saleratus is also used by them in considerable quantities.

But even where these adulterations are not practised, the bakers' bread is very rarely a wholesome article of diet.

If any dependence is to be placed on the testimony of several of the principal bakers and flour merchants in New York, Boston and other cities, the flour which most of our public bakers work into bread, is of a very inferior quality, to what is called good 'family flour', and for which they pay from one to three dollars less per barrel; and they sometimes purchase large quantities of old spoiled flour from New Orleans and elsewhere, which has heated and soured in the barrel, and perhaps become almost as solid as a mass of chalk; so that they are obliged to break it up, and grind it over, and spread it out, and expose it to the air, in order to purify it in a measure from its acid and other bad properties; and then they mix it with a portion of much better flour; and from this mixture they can make, as they say, the very largest and finest looking loaf. (An aged and very respectable member of the Society of Friends, in New York, who had long been extensively engaged in the flour business in that city, and who had always had his family bread made in his own house, was one day asked by his daughter, why he never used the baker's bread: – 'Because, my child,' replied he, 'I know what it is made of.') But should the public bakers always use the best of flour, their bread, as a general statement, would still be very inferior to well made domestic bread, in point of sweetness and wholesomeness. Their mode of manufacturing bread – to say the least of it – destroys much of the virtue of the flour or meal; and hence their bread is only palatable – even to those who are accustomed to it – within twelve, or at the longest, twenty-four hours after it is baked.

But I must repeat, that in making these statements, I am not prompted by any unkind feelings towards public bakers; I have no doubt that they are as honest in their calling as any other class of men; but perhaps there is no other class pursuing an interest founded on the necessities of their fellow creatures, whose expedients to increase the lucrativeness of their business, are so immediately and universally injurious to the health of those on whom they depend for support.

If any of my statements are thought to be exaggerated or incorrect, I can only say, that with honest and benevolent intentions, I have diligently sought for the truth; and if I have been in any respect betrayed into error, I have been misinformed by public bakers themselves, who certainly ought to know the truth in this matter; and who could have no conceivable reason for making the general character of their calling appear worse than it really is. Nevertheless, I have no question that there are individuals in every city employed as public bakers, who are too honest – too conscientious – too upright in heart, to be guilty of any practice which they consider fraudulent or improper.

Still, truth compels me to declare, that if we would have good and wholesome bread, it must be made within the precincts of our own domestic threshold; and by those whose skill and care are exercised more with a view to secure our health and happiness, than their own pecuniary interest.

Properties of Bread

Superfine flour injurious – a probable cause of some common disorders. Objections to coarse bread. Its medical properties. Extensive experiments of its use, by soldiers and others. Use among European peasantry. Selection, preservation and grinding of wheat.

Whether our bread is of domestic manufacture or made by the public baker, that which is made of superfine flour is always far less wholesome, in any and every situation of life, than that which is made of wheaten meal which contains ail the natural properties of the grain.

It is true, that when much flesh is eaten with our bread, or when bread constitutes but a very small and unimportant portion of our food, the injurious effects of superfine flour bread are not always so immediately and distinctly perceived as in other cases. Nevertheless, it is a general and invariable law of our nature, that all concentrated forms of food are unfriendly to the physiological or vital interests of our bodies.

A very large proportion of all the diseases and ailments in civic life, are originated by causes which are introduced into the alimentary canal as articles of diet; and disturbance and derangement of function – obstructions, debility and irritations, are among the most important elements of those diseases.

It is, probably, speaking within bounds to say that nine tenths of the adults, and nearly as large a proportion of youth in civic life, are more or less afflicted with obstructions and disturbances in the stomach and bowels, and other organs of the abdomen, the symptoms of which are either habitual costiveness or diarrhoea, or an alternation of both; or frequent and severe attacks of what are called bilious colics, &c., &c.; and in children and youth, worms, fits, convulsions, &c. And I cannot but feel confident, that the use of superfine flour bread is among the important causes of these and numerous other difficulties.

I have indeed been surprised to observe that in the hundreds of cases of chronic diseases of every form and name which have come to my knowledge within the last five or six years, costiveness of the bowels has in almost every instance been among the first and most important symptoms. And I have never known this difficulty, even after an obstinate continuance of five, ten, twenty or thirty years, fail to disappear in a short time, after the coarse wheaten bread of a proper character has been substituted for that made of superfine flour.

Some physicians and other individuals, without properly examining the subject, have raised several objections against the coarse wheaten bread.

It is said, in the first place, that bran is wholly indigestible, and therefore should never be taken into the human stomach.

This objection betrays so much ignorance of the final causes and constitutional laws, clearly indicated by the anatomical structure and physiological economy of the alimentary organs, that it scarcely deserves the slightest notice. If the digestive organs of man were designed to receive nothing but digestible and nutrient substances, they would have been constructed and arranged very differently from what they are. As we have already seen, everything which nature provides for our sustenance, consists of certain proportions of nutritious and innutritious matter; and a due proportion of innutritious matter in our food is as essential to the health and functional integrity of our alimentary organs, as a due proportion of nutritious matter is to the sustenance of the body.

Another objection is, that although bran may serve, like other mechanical irritants and excitants, for a while, to relieve constipation, yet it soon wears out the excitability of the organs and leaves them more inactive than before.

Here again, a false statement is urged by inexcusable ignorance; for it is not true that the bran acts in the manner supposed in this objection; nor are the effects here asserted ever produced by it.

It is true, however, that the very pernicious habits of some people, who use the coarse wheaten bread, entirely counteract the aperient effects of the bread; and it is true that others, depending wholly on the virtues of this bread for peristaltic action, and neglecting all exercise, by their extreme inertness, and indolence, and overeating, bring on a sluggishness, and debility, and constipation of the bowels, and perhaps become severely afflicted with piles, in spite of the natural fitness of the bread to promote regular peristaltic action, and to prevent all these results.

A third objection is that though the coarse wheaten bread may do very well for those who are troubled with constipation, by mechanically irritating and exciting the stomach and bowels, yet for that very reason it is wholly unfit and improper for those who are afflicted with chronic diarrhoea.

Here is still another objection founded in ignorance of the true physiological and pathological principles which it involves. The truth is that the coarse wheaten bread, under a proper general regimen, is as excellent and sure a remedy for chronic diarrhoea as for chronic constipation.

I have seen cases of chronic diarrhoea of the most obstinate character, and which had baffled the highest medical skill and every mode of treatment for more than twenty years, yielding entirely under a proper general regimen, in which this bread was the almost exclusive article of food, and not a particle of medicine was used. And I have never known such a mode of treatment to fail of wholly relieving diarrhoea, whether recent or chronic; although a very great number of cases have come under my notice.

It is fully evident, therefore, that the bran does not act on the digestive organs as a mere mechanical irritant; for if it did, it would always necessarily aggravate, rather than alleviate diarrhoea. Nor does it relieve diarrhoea on the principle of a narcotic nor of a stimulant; for the effect of these is always to give an immediate check to that complaint; and in such a manner as to expose the system to a return of it. But the coarse wheaten bread seems to increase the disease for a short time, at first, and then gradually restores the healthy condition and action of the bowels.

The mucilage of wheat bran is probably one of the most soothing substances in the vegetable kingdom, that can be applied to the mucous membrane of the stomach and bowels.

Chronic constipation and chronic diarrhoea both spring from the same root. Where the constitutional vigor of the alimentary canal is very considerable, continued irritations, resulting in debility, will produce constipation; and these continued causes operating for some time, will often induce such a state of debility and irritability as is attended with diarrhoea: – and in other cases, when this constitutional vigor of the alimentary canal is much less, diarrhoea is far more readily induced, and rendered chronic.

Coarse wheaten bread, then, by its adaptation to the anatomical structure and to the physiological properties and functional powers of our organs, serves to prevent and to remove the disorders and diseases of our bodies, only by preventing and removing irritation and morbid action and condition, and thereby affording the system an opportunity of recovering its healthy and vigorous action and condition. And the thousands of individuals in our own country of every age – of both sexes – of all situations, conditions and circumstances, who within the last six years have been benefited by using the coarse wheaten bread, instead of that made of superfine flour, are living witnesses of the virtues of that bread.

But the testimony in favor of coarse wheaten bread as an important article in the food of man, is by no means limited to our own country nor to modern times.

In all probability, as we have already seen, the first generations of our species, who became acquainted with the art of making bread, continued for many centuries to employ all the substance of the grain, which they coarsely mashed in their rude mortars or mills. And even since mankind began, by artificial means, to separate the bran from the flour, and to make bread from the latter, the more close and discerning observers among physicians and philanthropists, have perceived and asserted, that bread made of fine flour is decidedly less wholesome than that made of the unbolted wheat meal.

Hippocrates, styled the father of medicine, who flourished more than two thousand years ago, and who depended far more on a correct diet and general regimen, both for the prevention and removal of disease, than he did on medicine, particularly commended the unbolted wheat meal bread, 'for its salutary effects upon the bowels.' It was a fact well understood by the ancients, that this bread was much more conducive to the general health and vigor of their bodies, and every way better adapted to nourish and sustain them than that made of the fine flour. And accordingly, their wrestlers and others who were trained for great bodily power, 'ate only the coarse wheaten bread, to preserve them in their strength of limbs.' The Spartans were famous for this kind of bread; and we learn from Pliny that the Romans, as a nation, at that period of their history when they were the most remarkable for bodily vigor and personal prowess and achievement, knew no other bread for three hundred years. The warlike and powerful nations which overran the Roman Empire, and finally spread over the greater part of Europe, used no other kind of bread than that which was made of the whole substance of the grain; and from the fall of the Roman Empire to the present day, a large proportion of the inhabitants of all Europe and the greater part of Asia, have rarely used any other kind of bread.

'If you set any value on health, and have a mind to preserve nature,' – said Thomas Tryon, student in physic, in his *Way to Health, Long Life and Happiness*, published in London, in the latter part of the fifteenth century, 'you must not separate the finest from the coarsest flour; because that which is fine is naturally of an obstructive and stopping quality; but, on the contrary, the other, which is coarse, is of a cleansing and opening nature, therefore the bread is best which is made of both together. It is more wholesome, easier of digestion, and more strengthening than bread made of the finest flour. It must be confessed, that the nutrimentive quality is contained in the fine flour; yet, in the branny part is contained the opening and digestive quality; and there is as great a necessity for the one as the other, for the support of health: that which is accounted the worst is as good and beneficial to nature as the best; for when the finest flour is separated from the coarsest and branny parts, neither the one nor the other has the true operations of the wheat meal. The eating of fine bread, therefore, is inimical to health, and contrary both to nature and reason; and was at first invented to gratify wanton and luxurious persons, who are ignorant both of themselves, and the true virtue and efficacy of natural things.' 'Baron Steuben has often told me,' says Judge Peters, 'that the peculiar healthfulness of the Prussian soldiers, was in a great measure to be attributed to their ammunition bread, made of grain, triturated or ground, but not bolted; which was accounted the most wholesome and nutritious part of their rations. The Dutch sailors, in the days of their naval glory, were supplied with the same kind of bread.'

'During the war between England and France, near the close of the last century,' says Mr Samuel Prior, a respectable merchant of Salem, New Jersey – 'the crops of grain, and particularly wheat, were very small in England, and the supplies from Dantzic, the Netherlands and Sweden being cut off by the French army, and also the usual supplies from America failing, there was a very great scarcity of wheat in England. The British army was then very extensive, and it was exceedingly difficult to procure provisions for it, both at home and abroad – on land and sea. Such was the demand for the foreign army, and such the deficiency of crops at home and supplies from abroad, that serious fears were entertained that the army would suffer, and that the continental enterprise of the British government would be defeated in consequence of the scarcity of provisions; and every prudential measure by which such a disastrous event could be prevented was carefully considered and proposed. William Pitt was then prime minister of state, and at his instance, government recommended to the people generally throughout Great Britain, to substitute potatoes and rice as far as possible for bread, in order to save the wheat for the foreign army. This recommendation was promptly complied with by many of the people. But still the scarcity was alarmingly great. In this emergency, parliament passed a law (to take effect for two years) that the army at home should be supplied with bread made of unbolted wheat meal, solely for the purpose of making the wheat go as far as possible, and thus saving as much as they could from the home consumption, for the better supply of the army on the continent.

'Eighty thousand men were quartered in barracks in the counties of Essex and Suffolk. A great many were also quartered throughout the towns, at taverns, in squads of thirty or forty in a place. Throughout the whole of Great Britain, the soldiers were supplied with this coarse bread. It was deposited in the storerooms with the other provisions of the army; and on the day that it was baked, and at nine o'clock the next morning, was distributed to the soldiers – who were at first exceedingly displeased with the bread, and refused to eat it, often casting it from them with great rage, and violent execrations. But after two or three weeks they began to be much pleased with it, and preferred it to the fine flour bread.

'My father,' continues Mr P., 'whom I have often heard talk these things over, was a miller and a baker, and resided in the county of Essex, on the border joining Suffolk, and near the barracks containing the eighty thousand soldiers. He contracted with government to supply the eastern district of the county of Essex with the kind of bread I have mentioned; and he used always to send me with it to the depositories on the day it was baked; and though I was then a youth, I can still very distinctly remember the angry looks and remarks of the soldiers, when they were first supplied with it. Indeed they often threw their loaves at me as I passed along, and accompanied them with a volley of curses. The result of this experiment was that not only the wheat was made to go much farther, but the health of the soldiers improved so much and so manifestly, in the course of a few months, that it became a matter of common remark among themselves, and of observation and surprise among the officers and physicians of the army. These gentlemen at length came out with confidence and zeal on the subject, and publicly declared that the soldiers were never before so healthy and robust; and that disease of every kind had almost entirely disappeared from the army. The public papers were for months filled with recommendations of this bread, and the civic physicians almost universally throughout Great Britain pronounced it far the most healthy bread that could be eaten, and as such, recommended it to all the people, who very extensively followed the advice: – and the coarse wheaten bread was very generally introduced into families, female boarding schools, and indeed all public institutions. The nobility also generally used it; and in fact, in many towns, it was a rare thing to meet with a piece of fine flour bread. The physicians generally asserted that this wheaten bread was the very best thing that could be taken into the human stomach, to promote digestion and peristaltic action; and that it, more than anything else, would assist the stomach in digesting other things which were less easily digested, and therefore they recommend that a portion of it should be eaten at every meal with other food.

'Still, after this extensive experiment had been made with such happy results, and after so general and full a testimony had been given in favor of the coarse wheaten bread, when large supplies of superfine flour came in from America, and the crops at home were abundant, and the act of parliament in relation to the army became extinct, most of the people who had before been accustomed to the use of fine flour bread, now by degrees returned again to their old habits of eating fine bread. Many of the nobility, however, continued to use the coarse bread for a number of years afterwards. General Hanoward, Squire Western, Squire Hanbury and others living near my father's, continued to use the bread for a long time, and some of them still used it when I left home and came to America, in 1816.'

The testimony of sea captains and old whalemen is equally in favor of wheaten bread. 'I have always found,' said a very intelligent sea captain of more than thirty years' experience, 'that the coarser my ship bread, the healthier my crew is.' A writer in *Rees' Cyclopaedia* (article Bread) says – 'The inhabitants of Westphalia, who are a hardy and robust people, and capable of enduring the greatest fatigues, are a living testimony to the salutary effects of this sort of bread; and it is remarkable that they are very seldom attacked by acute fevers, and those other diseases which are from bad humors.'

In short, as I have already stated, the bread of a large portion of the laboring class, or peasantry, throughout Europe, Asia and Africa, and the islands of the ocean, whether leavened or unleavened – whether more or less artificially prepared, is made of the whole substance of the grain from which it is manufactured; and no one who is sufficiently enlightened in physiological science to qualify him to judge correctly in this matter can doubt that bread made in the best manner from unbolted wheat meal is far better adapted to the anatomical structure and physiological powers of the alimentary organs of man, than bread made of superfine wheat flour; and consequently, the former is far more conducive to the health and vigor and general well-being of man than the latter.

If, therefore, mankind will have raised bread which in every respect most perfectly conforms to the laws of constitution and relation established in their nature, and is most highly conducive to the welfare of their bodies and souls, then must it be well made, well baked, light and sweet bread, which contains all the natural properties of the wheat. And if they will have this bread of the very best, and most wholesome kind, they must, as I have already stated, see that the soil from which their wheat is raised is of a proper character, and is properly tilled – that the wheat is plump – full-grown – ripe, and free from rust and other diseases; and then, before it is ground, they must see that it is thoroughly cleansed, not only from chaff, cockles, tares, and such like substances, but also from all smut, and every kind of impurity that may be attached to the skin of the kernel. And let every one be assured that this is a matter which really deserves all the attention and care that I suggest.

If human existence is worth possessing, it is worth preserving; and they who have enjoyed it as some have done, and as all the human family are naturally endowed with the capabilities to enjoy it, certainly will not doubt whether it is worth possessing; nor, if they will properly consider the matter, can they doubt that its preservation is worthy of their most serious and diligent care.

And when they perceive how intimately and closely the character of their bread is connected with the dearest interests of man, they will not be inclined to feel that any reasonable amount of care and labor is too much to be given to secure precisely the right kind of bread.

I repeat, then, that they who would have the very best bread should certainly wash their wheat, and cleanse it thoroughly from all impurities, before they take it to the mill; and when it is properly dried, it should be ground by sharp stones which will cut rather than mash it: and particular care should be taken that it is not ground too fine. Coarsely ground wheat meal, even when the bran is retained, makes decidedly sweeter and more wholesome bread than very finely ground meal. When the meal is ground, it should immediately be spread out to cool before it is put into sacks or casks: – for if it is packed or enclosed in a heated state, it will be far more likely to become sour and musty. And I say again, where families are in circumstances to do wholly as they choose in the matter, it is best to have but little ground at a time; as the freshly ground meal is always the liveliest and sweetest, and makes the most delicious bread.

When the meal is thus prepared and brought home, whether in a barrel or sack, the next thing to be attended to, is, that it be placed and kept in a perfectly clean, and sweet, and well ventilated meal room. It should on no consideration be put into a closet, or pantry, or store-room, which is seldom aired, and more rarely cleansed; and into which all manner of rubbish is thrown; or even where other kinds of provisions are kept. If the meal be put into a pantry or store-room which is confined and dirty, and into which old boots and shoes, and old clothes and pieces of carpet, and other things of this kind, are thrown – or where portions of vegetable or animal substance, whether cooked or uncooked, are habitually or even occasionally put and permitted to remain, it must be expected, as a matter of course, of necessity, that the quality of the meal will be considerably deteriorated by the impurities with which the air of the place will be loaded, and which will be continually generated there.

People generally have but a sorry idea of what constitutes true cleanliness; but they may be assured that they cannot be too deeply impressed with the importance of keeping their meal room as clean and sweet and well aired as possible.

Fermentation

Chemical composition of flour. Yeast – modes of preparing it. Substitutes for it. Fermentation, and its products. Vinous, acetous and putrefactive fermentation.

Having procured good wheat, cleansed it thoroughly, and got it properly ground, and placed in the meal room, the next step is to take a portion of the meal and manufacture it into good bread. But in order that this may be done in the most certain and perfect manner, it is important that the properties of the meal and the principles concerned in breadmaking should be well understood.

According to the statement of Prof. Thomson, of Edinburgh, one pound of good wheat meal contains ten ounces of farina or starch, three ounces of bran, six drams of gluten and two drams of sugar; and it is because wheat contains such proportions of these substances that it makes the very best loaf bread. The farina or starch is the principal nourishing property; the saccharine matter or sugar is also highly nutrient; but in the process of making loaf bread, it serves mainly, by its vinous fermentation, to produce the gas or air by which the dough is raised and the bread made light. The gluten is likewise a very nutrient property, but in loaf bread, it principally serves, by its cohesiveness, like gum elastic, or India rubber, to prevent the gas or air formed by the fermentation of the sugar, from escaping or passing off; and the gas being thus retained, inflates or puffs up the dough, and makes it porous and light. The bran, with its mucilaginous and other properties, not only adds to the nutritiousness of the bread, but eminently serves to increase its digestibility, and to invigorate the digestive organs, and preserve the general integrity of their functions.

The wheat which is raised in Virginia, and the southern states generally, contains a larger proportion of gluten than that which is raised in the western part of the state of New York. Hence bakers are able to make a larger loaf of bread out of a pound of southern flour than they can out of a pound of western flour; and consequently some of them have endeavored to make their customers believe that the southern flour is the most profitable. It certainly is the most profitable for the baker; but it is not the most profitable for the consumer.

The next thing indispensably necessary to the making of good bread, is good lively sweet yeast, or leaven, to produce what is called the panary, or more properly, the vinous fermentation of the saccharine matter, or sugar.

Some bread-makers will do best with one kind of yeast or leaven, and some with another. I have generally found that people do best with those materials to which they have been most accustomed; but I am sorry to find so general a dependence on breweries for yeast. To say nothing of the impure and poisonous substances which brewers employ in the manufacture of beer, and which always affect the quality of their yeast, I am confident that domestic yeast can be made of a far superior quality. However light and good in other respects that bread may be which is made with brewers' yeast, I have rarely if ever seen any in which I could not at once detect the disagreeable properties of the yeast.

There are various ways of making domestic yeast. One of the simplest, and perhaps the best, is the following, which was communicated to me by one of the best breadmakers I ever saw:

> Put into one gallon of water a double handful of hops; boil them fifteen or twenty minutes, then strain off the water while it is scalding hot; stir in wheat flour or meal till it becomes a thick batter, so that it will hardly pour; let it stand till it becomes about blood warm, then add a pint of good lively yeast, and stir it well; and then let it stand in a place where it will be kept at a temperature of about 70° F till it becomes perfectly light, whether more or less time is required; and then it is fit for use; or if it is desired to keep a portion of it, let it stand several hours and become cool; and then put it into a clean jug and cork it tight, and place it in the cellar where it will keep cool; and it may be preserved good, ten or twelve days, and even longer.

Another way by which yeast when thus made may be preserved much longer, and perhaps more conveniently, is, to take it when it has become perfectly light, and stir in good indian meal until it becomes a hard dough; then take this dough and make it into small thin cakes, and dry them perfectly, without baking or cooking them at all. These cakes, if kept perfectly dry, will be good for several weeks and even months.

When yeast is needed, take some of these cakes (more or less according to the quantity of bread desired) and break them fine and dissolve them in warm water, and then stir in some wheat flour till a batter is formed, which should be kept at a temperature of about 60° F till the yeast becomes light and lively, and fitted for making bread.

Others, in making this yeast, originally put into the water with the hops, a double handful of good clean wheat bran, and boil them up together and strain off the water as above described: others again, boil up a quantity of wheat bran without the hops, and make their yeast in all other respects as above described.

The milk yeast is greatly preferred by many; and when it is well managed, it certainly makes very handsome bread. The way of making it is simple. Take a quart of milk fresh from the cow, (more or less according to the quantity of bread desired), a little salt is generally added, and some add about half a pint of water blood warm, but this is not essential; then stir wheat flour or meal into the milk till it forms a moderately thick batter; and then cover it over, and place it where it will remain at a temperature of from 60° to 70° F till it becomes perfectly light. It should then be used immediately: and let it be remembered that dough made with this yeast will sour sooner than that made with other yeast; and also that the bread after it is baked will become extremely dry and *crumbly* much sooner than bread made with other yeast. Yet this bread, when a day old, is exceedingly light and beautiful: albeit some dislike the animal smell and taste which it derives from the milk.

In all these preparations of yeast and dough, it should ever be recollected that 'the process of fermentation cannot go on when the temperature is below 30° F, that it proceeds quite slowly at 50°, moderately at 60°, rapidly at 70°, and very rapidly at 80°.'

If, therefore, it is desired to have the yeast or dough stand several hours before it is used or baked, it should be kept at a temperature of about 50°. But in the ordinary way of making bread, a temperature varying from 60° to 70°, or about summer heat, is perhaps as near right as it can well be made.

Prof. Thomson gives the following directions for making yeast in large quantities:

Add ten pounds of flour to two gallons of boiling water; – stir it well into a paste, let this mixture stand for seven hours, and then add about a quart of good yeast In about six or eight hours, this mixture, if kept in a warm place, will have fermented and produced as much yeast as will make 120 quartern loaves (of 4 lbs each.)

A much smaller quantity can be made by observing due proportions of the ingredients.

To raise bread in a very short time without yeast, Prof. Thomson gives the following recipe:

Dissolve in water 2 ounces, 5 drams and 45 grains of common crystallized carbonate of soda, and mix the solution well with your dough, and then add 7 ounces, 2 drams and 22 grains of muriatic acid of the specific gravity of 1,121, and knead it as rapidly as possible with your dough; it will rise immediately – fully as much, if not more than dough mixed with yeast – and when baked, will be a very light and excellent bread.

Smaller quantities would be required for small batches of bread.

A tea-spoonful or more (according to the quantity of dough or batter) of supercarbonate of soda dissolved in water, and flour stirred in till it becomes a batter, and then an equal quantity of tartaric acid dissolved and stirred in thoroughly, will in a few minutes make very light batter for griddle or pancakes; or if it be mixed into a thick dough, it will make light bread.

Good lively yeast, however, makes better bread than these alkalies and acids: howbeit these are very convenient in emergencies, when bread or cakes must be prepared in a very short time; or when the yeast has proved inefficient.

We see then that wheat meal consists of certain proportions of starch, gluten, sugar, bran, &c.; and that in making loaf bread we add yeast or leaven in order to produce that kind of fermentation peculiar to saccharine matter or sugar, which is called vinous, and by which the gas or air is formed that raises the dough. But the sugar is an incorporate part of every particle of the meal, and is therefore equally diffused throughout the whole mass; and hence if we would make the very best loaf bread, the fermentive principle or yeast must also be equally diffused throughout the whole mass, so that a suitable portion of yeast will be brought to act at the same time on every particle of saccharine matter in the mass.

But let us endeavor to understand this process of fermentation. To speak in the language of chemistry, sugar is composed of certain proportions of carbon, oxygen and hydrogen. The yeast, acting on the sugar, overcomes those affinities by which these substances are held in the

Ticket Number

A - 709

Receipt of Purchase

Romney, Hythe and Dymchurch Railway

New Romney Railway Shop
www.rhdr.org.uk
info@rhdr.org.uk

Items

Product	Price	Qty	Total
BookBREADMAKING type		1	£3.99
name of book here			

Total Qty 1

Sub Total	£3.99
Date	07/06/2019 10 54 33
Staff	Peter B
Device	NR Shop Till 1
Total	£3.99

Tenders
Cash   £3.99
- Change   £0.00

Tax Summary

Name	Perc	Tax
No Tax	0%	£0.00
Total		£0.00

VAT Number 202 0175 54

Return of Green Goddess – Sunday 9th June –
pre-book your tickets. www.rhdr.org.uk

RECBOOKBHDMVWSL6NP08

constitutional arrangement of sugar, and the process of decay or decomposition of the sugar takes place, which is called vinous fermentation. By this process of decay, two other forms of matter are produced, of an essentially different nature from each other and from the sugar. One of them is called carbonic acid gas or air, being formed by a chemical combination of certain proportions of carbon and oxygen. The other is known by the name of alcohol, and consists of a chemical combination of certain proportions of carbon, oxygen, and hydrogen. Carbonic acid gas is also produced by animal respiration or breathing, by the combustion of wood, coal, &c. &c. and in other ways of nature and of art: but neither in nature nor in art is there any known way by which alcohol can be produced, except by that process of the decay or destruction of sugar called vinous fermentation.

The carbonic acid gas, produced in the manner I have stated, is the air which inflates or puffs up and swells out the bread, when there is sufficient gluten or other cohesive matter in the dough to prevent its escape.

If the dough be permitted to stand too long in a warm place, the fermentation, having destroyed most or all of the sugar, will begin to act on the starch and mucilage, and destroy their nature, and produce vinegar; and therefore this stage of it is called the acetous fermentation: and if it still be permitted to go on, it will next commence its work of destruction on the gluten; and this is called the putrefactive fermentation, because it in many respects resembles the putrefaction of animal matter.

The vinous fermentation, therefore, by which the dough is raised and made light, may be carried to all necessary extent, and still be limited in its action to the saccharine matter or sugar – leaving the starch and gluten, and other properties of the meal, uninjured; and this is the point at which the fermentation should be arrested by the heat that bakes the dough. If it be permitted to go beyond the sugar, and act on the mucilage and starch, and produce acidity, the excellence of the bread is in some degree irreparably destroyed. The acid may be neutralized by pearlash or soda, so that the bread shall not be sour; but still, something of the natural flavor of the bread is gone, and it is not possible by any earthly means to restore it; and this injury will always be in proportion to the extent to which the process of the acetous fermentation is permitted to go in destroying the nature of the starch, and the bread will be proportionably destitute of that natural sweetness and delicious richness essential to good bread. Yet it is almost universally true, both in public and domestic breadmaking, that the acetous fermentation is allowed to take place; and saleratus, or soda, or some other chemical agent is employed to neutralize the acid. By this means we may have bread free from acidity, it is true, but it is also destitute of the best and most delicious properties of good bread and generally, by the time it is twenty-four hours old – and this is particularly true of bakers' bread – it is as dry and tasteless and unsavory as if it were made of plaster of Paris.

Many breadmakers mix their saleratus or soda with their yeast, or introduce it when they mix their dough, so that if the acetous fermentation does take place, the acid is neutralized by the alkali, and therefore, not being perceived, it is supposed never to have existed, and the bread is called sweet and good; especially if a small quantity of molasses be employed in making the dough. Others far more wisely withhold their alkali till the dough is raised enough to mould into the loaf, and then if it is found to be in any degree acid, a solution of saleratus or soda is worked into it, so as just to neutralize the acid, and no more. This is infinitely better than to have sour bread, which, after all, is almost everywhere met with; yet the very best bread that can be made in this way is only second best. Happy are they who can make good, light and sweet bread, without the use of molasses – without suffering the least degree of acetous fermentation to take place, and without employing saleratus, soda, or any other kind of alkali.

The third or putrefactive stage of fermentation rarely takes place in domestic breadmaking; but it is by no means uncommon in public bakeries. Indeed it is thought necessary in the manufacture of certain kinds of crackers, in order to make them split open, and render them brittle, and cause them readily to become soft when dipped into water. But dyspepsia crackers, and all other kinds of bread made in this way are, to say the least of them, miserable stuff. For besides the fact that all the best qualities of the flour or meal have been destroyed by fermentation, the great quantity of alkali employed in neutralizing the acid is necessarily injurious to the digestive organs.

Preparation of Bread

Mixing. Much kneading necessary. Rising, or fermentation. Use of alkalies, saleratus and soda. Baking. Ovens. Alcohol in bread. Preservation of bread.

Now, then, the business of the breadmaker is, to take the wheat meal, prepared in the manner I have stated, and with all the properties I have described, and convert it into good, light, sweet, well-baked bread, with the least possible change in those properties; so that the bread, when done, will present to the senses of smell and taste, all the delicious flavor and delicate sweetness which pure organs perceive in the meal of good new wheat, just taken from the ear and ground, or chewed without grinding; and it should be so baked that it will, as a general statement, require and secure a full exercise of the teeth in mastication.

In order to this, as we have seen, it is necessary, in the first place, that the wheat should be of the best kind, and well cleansed, and the meal properly prepared. In the next place, it is necessary that the yeast should be fresh, lively and sweet; and in the third place, it is necessary that the dough should be properly mixed, raised and baked.

Take then such a quantity of meal, in a perfectly clean and sweet bread trough, as is necessary for the quantity of bread desired, and having made a hollow in the centre, turn in as much yeast as a judgment matured by sound experience shall deem requisite; then add such a quantity of water, milk and water, or clear milk, as is necessary to form the meal into a dough of proper consistency. Some prefer bread mixed with water alone; others prefer that which is mixed with milk and water; and others think that bread mixed with good milk is much richer and better; while others dislike the animal odor and taste of bread mixed with milk. Perhaps the very best and most wholesome bread is that which is mixed with pure soft water, when such bread is made perfect. But whether water, milk and water, or milk alone is employed, it should be used at a temperature of about blood heat.

Here let it be understood that the starch of the meal is of such a nature that, by a delicate process peculiar to itself, it becomes changed into sugar or saccharine matter; and when the fluid used in mixing the dough is of a proper temperature, and the dough is properly mixed and kneaded, this process, to some small extent, takes place, and a small portion of the starch is actually converted into sugar, and thereby increases the sweetness of the bread. Let it also be recollected here, that the saccharine matter on which the yeast is to act, is equally diffused throughout the whole mass of the meal; and therefore if the yeast be not properly diffused throughout the whole mass, but is unequally distributed, so that an undue quantity of it remains in one part, while other parts receive little or none, then the fermentation will go on very rapidly in some parts of the mass, and soon run into the acetous state, while in other parts it will proceed very slowly or not at all; and consequently large cavities will be formed in some parts of the dough, while other parts of it will remain as compact and heavy as when first mixed, and sometimes even more so. I need not say that such dough cannot be made into good bread; yet it is probably true, that more than nine tenths of the bread consumed in this country is more or less of this character. Nor, after what I have said, should it seem necessary for me to remark, that good bread cannot be made by merely stirring the meal, and yeast, and water or milk together into a thin dough or sponge, and suffering it to ferment with little or no working or kneading. Bread made in this manner, if it is not full of cavities large enough for a mouse to burrow in, surrounded by parts as solid as lead, is almost invariably full of cells of the size of large peas and grapes; and the substance of the bread has a shining, glutinous appearance; and if the bread is not sour, it is because pearlash or some other kind of alkali has been used to destroy the acid.

The very appearance of such bread is forbidding, and shows, at a glance, that it has not been properly mixed – that the yeast has acted unequally on different portions of the meal, and that the fermentation has not been of the right kind.

But if the yeast be so diffused throughout the whole mass, as that a suitable portion of it will act on each and every particle of the saccharine matter at the same time, and if the dough be of such a consistency and temperature as not to admit of too rapid a fermentation, then each minute portion of saccharine matter throughout the whole mass will, in the process of fermentation, produce its little volume of air, which will form its little cell, about the size of a pin's head, and smaller; and this will take place so nearly at the same time, in every part of the dough, that the whole will be raised and made as light as a sponge, before the acetous fermentation takes place in any part. And then if it be properly moulded and baked, it will make the most beautiful and delicious bread – perfectly light and sweet, without the use of any alkali, and with all the gluten and nearly all the starch of the meal remaining unchanged by fermentation.

Proper materials, proper care, a due amount of labor, a suitable length of time, and proper temperature, are all, therefore, necessary to the making of good bread.

With your meal, and yeast, and water or milk brought together before you, then, proceed in the light of the instruction you have now received, to mix your dough; and remember that the more thoroughly you knead it, the more equally you diffuse the yeast throughout the whole mass, and bring it to act on every particle of the saccharine matter at the same time, and the whiter, lighter, and more delicious you make your bread.

Who that can look back thirty or forty years to those blessed days of New England's prosperity and happiness, when our good mothers used to make the family bread, but can well remember how long and how patiently those excellent matrons stood over their bread troughs, kneading and moulding their dough? and who with such recollections cannot also well remember the delicious bread that these mothers used invariably to set before them? There was a natural sweetness and richness in it which made it always desirable; and which we cannot now vividly recollect, without feeling a strong desire to partake again of such bread as our mothers made for us in the days of our childhood.

Let it be borne in mind, then, that without a very thorough kneading of the dough, there can be no just ground of confidence that the bread will be good. 'It should be kneaded,' says one of much experience in this matter, 'till it becomes flaky.' Indeed I am confident that our loaf bread would be greatly improved in all its qualities, if the dough were for a considerable time subjected to the operations of the machine which the bakers call the break, used in making crackers and sea-bread.

The wheat meal, and especially if it is ground coarsely, swells considerably in the dough, and therefore the dough should not, at first, be made quite so stiff, as that made of superfine flour; and when it is raised, if it is found too soft to mould well, let a little more meal be added.

When the dough has been properly mixed and thoroughly kneaded, cover it over with a clean napkin or towel, and a light woollen blanket kept for the purpose, and place the bread trough where the temperature will be kept at about 60° F, or about summer heat, and there let it remain till the dough becomes light. But as it is impossible to regulate the quantity and quality of your yeast, the moisture and temperature of your dough, and several other conditions and circumstances, so as to secure at all times precisely the same results in the same time, it is therefore necessary that careful attention should be given that the proper moment should be seized to work over and mould the dough into the loaf, and get it into the oven, just at the time when it is as light as it can be made by the vinous fermentation, and before the acetous fermentation commences.

If, however, by any means there should unfortunately be a little acidity in the dough, take a small quantity of saleratus, or, what is better, carbonate of soda, and dissolve it in some warm water, and carefully work in just enough to neutralize the acid. The best breadmakers are so exceedingly careful on this point, that they dip their fingers into the solution of saleratus or soda, and thrust them into the dough in every part, as they work it over, so as to be sure that they get in just enough to neutralize the acid, and not a particle more.

I must here repeat, that they who would have the very best of bread, must always consider it a cause of regret, that there should be any necessity to use alkali; because the acetous fermentation cannot in any degree take place, without commensurately and irremediably impairing the quality of the bread. And here it should be remarked, that dough made of wheat meal will take on the acetous fermentation, or become sour, sooner than that made of fine flour. This is probably owing principally to the mucilage contained in the bran, which runs into the acetous fermentation sooner than starch.

While the dough is rising, preparations should be made for baking it. Some bake their bread in a brick oven, some in a stove, some in a reflector, and some in a baking kettle. In all these ways very good bread may be baked; but the baking kettle is decidedly the most objectionable. Probably there is no better and more certain way of baking bread well than in the use of the brick oven. Good breadmakers, accustomed to brick ovens, can always manage them with a very great degree of certainty; and as a general fact, bread is sweeter, baked in this way, than in any other. Yet, when it is well baked in tin reflectors, it is certainly very fine; and so it is also when well baked in iron stoves. But the baking of bread requires almost as much care and judgment as any part of the process of breadmaking. If the oven is too hot, the bread will burn on the outside before it is done in the centre; if it is too cold, the bread will be heavy, raw and sour. If the heat is much greater from below than from above, the bottom of the loaf will burn before the top is done: or if the heat is much greater from above than from below, the top of the loaf will burn before the bottom is done.

All these points therefore must be carefully attended to; and no small excuse ought to be considered a satisfactory apology for sour, heavy, raw or burnt bread; for it is hardly possible to conceive of an absolute necessity for such results; and the cases are extremely rare in which they are not the offspring of downright and culpable carelessness.

The best breadmakers I have ever known watch over their bread troughs while their dough is rising, and over their ovens while it is baking, with about as much care and attention as a mother watches over the cradle of her sick child.

Dough made of wheat meal requires a hotter oven than that made of fine flour; and it needs to remain in the oven longer. Indeed, it is a general fault of bread of every description, made in this country, that it is not sufficiently baked. Multitudes eat their bread hot and smoking from the oven in a half-cooked state; and very few seem to think there is any impropriety in doing so. But they who would have their bread good, not only a few hours after it comes from the oven, but as long as it can be kept, must see that it is thoroughly baked.

I have said that the process of vinous fermentation converts a portion of the saccharine matter of the meal into carbonic acid gas or air, by which means the dough is raised and made light; and that the same process converts a portion of the saccharine matter into alcohol. The alcohol thus generated is mostly if not entirely driven off by the heat of the oven when the dough is baking; and in modern times, ovens have been so constructed in England, as to serve the double purpose of ovens and stills; so that while the bread is baking, the alcohol is distilled off and condensed, and saved for the various uses of arts and manufacture.

The question has, however, been frequently started, whether a portion of the alcohol thus generated, is not contained in the bread when it comes from the oven.

This question cannot be answered with entire certainty; but there are some facts in relation to it of considerable importance.

It is perfectly certain that if two portions of wheat meal or flour be taken from the same barrel or sack, and one portion be made into unleavened bread, and the other portion be made into the very best fermented or raised bread, and both be eaten as soon as they are baked, the fermented bread will digest with more difficulty, and oppress and disturb the stomach more than the unleavened bread will. Indeed it is well known and very generally understood, that few of the articles which compose the food of man in civic life, are so trying to the human stomach, and so powerful causes of dyspepsia, as fresh-baked raised bread.

It is now well known also that alcohol wholly resists the action of the solvent fluid of the stomach, and is entirely indigestible; and always retards the digestion of those substances which contain it. How far all this may be true of carbonic acid gas, is not yet ascertained; but it is difficult to account for the difference between leavened and unleavened bread, as above stated, without supposing that the alcohol or carbonic acid gas, or both of them, are in some degree concerned in rendering the leavened bread, when newly baked, peculiarly oppressive and injurious to the stomach.

This, be it remembered, is purely a conjecture of my own; and I am not entirely certain that it is correct; but I see no other way of meeting the difficulty.

Be it as it may, however, it is very certain that when the bread has been drawn from the oven, and permitted to stand in a proper place twenty-four hours, either by evaporation or some other means, it becomes perfectly matured, and so changed in character, that it is, if properly made, one of the most wholesome articles entering into the diet of man; and at that age, there is not the slightest reason to believe that a particle of alcohol remains in the bread.

When therefore the bread is thoroughly baked, let it be taken from the oven and placed on a perfectly clean and sweet shelf, in a perfectly clean and well ventilated pantry. Do not, as you value the character of your bread, put it into a pantry where you set away dishes of cold meat, cold potatoes, and other vegetables, and keep your butter, cheese and various other table provisions – in a pantry which perhaps is seldom thoroughly cleansed with hot water and soap, and where the pure air of heaven seldom if ever has a free circulation. The quality of your bread should be of too much importance to allow of such reprehensible carelessness, not to say sluttishness. And if you will have your bread such as every one ought to desire to have it, you must pay the strictest attention to the cleanliness and sweetness of the place where you keep it.

If in baking, the outer crust should become a little too dry and crispy, you can easily remedy this by throwing a clean bread or table cloth over it for a short time when it first comes from the oven; but if this is not necessary, let the bread stand on an airy shelf, till it becomes perfectly cool, and when it is twenty-four hours old, it is fit for use; and if it is in all respects properly made, and properly kept, it will continue to be sweet and delicious bread for two or even three weeks, except perhaps in very hot and sultry weather.

When we have acquired the art of making such bread as I have described, in the very best manner, then have we carried the art of cooking to the very height of perfection; for it is not only true that there is no other artificially prepared article in human diet of so much importance as bread, but it is also true that there is no other preparation in the whole round of cooking, which requires so much care, and attention, and experience, and skill, and wisdom.

Who Should Make Bread

Making bread by rule. Bakers. Domestics. Sour bread. An anecdote. Mrs Van Winkle. Bad bread need not be made. How cake is made. Bread-making a drudgery. Excellent example of a mother. Eating bad bread. Importance of having good bread.

Who then shall make our bread? For after all that science in its utmost accuracy can do, in ascertaining principles and in laying down rules, there is little certainty that any one, who undertakes to make bread merely by rule, will be anything like uniformly successful. We may make a batch of bread according to certain rules, and it may prove excellent; and then we may make another batch according to the same rules, which may be very poor. For if we follow our rules ever so closely, there may be some slight differences in the quality or condition of the meal or the yeast, or something else, which will materially alter the character of the bread, if we do not exercise a proper care and judgment, and vary our operations according as the particular circumstances of the case may require.

Correct rules are certainly very valuable; but they can only serve as general way-marks in the art of breadmaking. Uniform success can only be secured by the exercise of that mature judgment which is always able to dictate those extemporaneous measures which every exigency and circumstance may require; and such a judgment can only result from a care and attention and experience which are the offspring of that moral sensibility which duly appreciates the importance of the quality of bread, in relation to the happiness and welfare of those that consume it.

But are we to look for such a sensibility in public bakers? Can we expect that they will feel so lively and so strong an interest for our enjoyment and for our physical and intellectual and moral wellbeing, that they will exercise all that care and attention and patience, and watch with that untiring vigilance and solicitude in all the progress of their operations, which are indispensably necessary in order to secure us the best of bread?

Or can we reasonably expect to find these qualifications in domestics – in those who serve us for hire? Many a female domestic, it is true, can make much better bread than her mistress can. Many a female domestic has an honest and sincere desire to do her duty faithfully; but can she be actuated by those sensibilities and affections which alone can secure that careful attention, that soundness of judgment, that accuracy of operation, without which the best of bread cannot uniformly, if ever, be produced?

No; it is the wife, the mother only – she who loves her husband and her children as woman ought to love, and who rightly perceives the relations between the dietetic habits and physical and moral condition of her loved ones, and justly appreciates the importance of good bread to their physical and moral welfare – she alone it is, who will be ever inspired by that cordial and unremitting affection and solicitude which will excite the vigilance, secure the attention, and prompt the action requisite to success, and essential to the attainment of that maturity of judgment and skillfulness of operation, which are the indispensable attributes of a perfect breadmaker. And could wives and mothers fully comprehend the importance of good bread in relation to all the bodily and intellectual and moral interests of their husbands and children, and in relation to the domestic and social and civil welfare of mankind, and to their religious prosperity, both for time and eternity, they would estimate the art and duty of breadmaking far, very far more highly than they now do. They would then realize that, as no one can feel so deep and delicate an interest for their husbands' and children's happiness as they do, so no one can be so proper a person to prepare for them that portion of their aliment, which requires a degree of care and attention that can only spring from the lively affections and solicitude of a wife and mother.

But it is a common thing to hear women say – 'We cannot always have good bread, if we take ever so much pains; it will sometimes be heavy, and sometimes be sour, and sometimes badly baked, in spite of all our care.'

It may be true that such things will sometimes happen, even with the best of care; but I believe that there is almost infinitely more poor bread than there is any good excuse for. The truth is, the quality of bread is a matter of too little consideration; and therefore too little care is given to the making of it. Moreover, the sense of taste is so easily vitiated, that we can very easily become reconciled to the most offensive gustatory qualities, and even learn to love them; and it is a very common thing to find families so accustomed to sour bread, that they have no perception of its acid quality.

'It is very strange,' said a lady to me one day at her dinner table, 'that some folks always have sour bread, and never know it.' She then went on to name a number of families in the circle of her acquaintance, who, she said, invariably had sour bread upon their tables when she visited them – 'and they never,' continued she, 'seem to have the least consciousness that their bread is not perfectly sweet and good.'

Yet this very lady, at the very moment she was thus addressing me, had sour bread upon her own table; and although I had for many months been very frequently at her table, I had never found any but sour bread upon it. Still she was wholly unconscious of the fact.

Difficult however as most women think it is, to have good bread always, yet there are some women who invariably have excellent bread. I have known such women. The wife of Thomans Van Winkle, Esq. of the beautiful valley of Booneton, New Jersey – peace to her ashes! – was deservedly celebrated throughout the whole circle of her acquaintance for her excellent bread. Few ever ate at her hospitable board once that did not desire to enjoy the privilege again. I know not how often it has been my good fortune to sit at her table; but the times have not been few; and though long past, and she who presided there has slept for years in her grave, yet the remembrance of those times and of those hospitalities, awakens in my bosom a deep and fervent sentiment of gratitude while I write.

Never at the table of Mrs Van Winkle did I eat poor bread; and of my numerous acquaintances who had sat at her table,

I never heard one say he had eaten poor bread there. Her bread was invariably good. Nay, it was of such a quality that it was impossible for any one to eat of it, and not be conscious that he was partaking of bread of extraordinary excellence.

Mrs Van Winkle, said I to her one day, while I was feasting on her delicious bread, tell me truly, is there either a miracle or mystery in this matter of breadmaking, by which you are enabled to have such excellent bread upon your table at all times, while I rarely ever find bread equally good at any other table, and at ninety-nine tables in a hundred, I almost invariably find poor bread? Is it necessarily so? Is it not possible for people by any means to have good bread uniformly?

'There is no necessity for having poor bread at any time, if those who make it will give proper care and attention to their business,' replied Mrs Van Winkle, confidently. 'The truth is,' continued she, 'most people attach very little importance to the quality of their bread; and therefore they give little care to the preparation of it. If every woman would see that her flour is sweet and good, that her yeast is fresh and lively, that her bread trough is kept perfectly clean and sweet, that her dough is properly mixed and thoroughly kneaded, and kept at a proper temperature, and at the proper time moulded into the loaf, and put into the oven, which has been properly heated, and there properly baked, then good bread would be as common as poor bread now is. But while there is such perfect carelessness and negligence about the matter, it is not surprising that bread should be generally poor.'

Mrs Van Winkle was undoubtedly correct. If anything like the care were given to breadmaking that its real importance demands, a loaf of poor bread would rarely be met with. Indeed, if the same degree of care were given to breadmaking, that is devoted to the making of cakes and pastry, we should far more generally be blessed with good bread.

Who does not know, that as soon as girls are old enough to go into company and to give parties, they begin to notice with great interest the qualities of the different kinds of cake and pastry which they meet with; and whenever they find anything very nice, they are exceedingly curious to learn precisely how it was made. And lest memory should be treacherous, they will carefully write down the exact rules for mixing and cooking it; 'so many pounds of flour, so many pounds of butter, so many pounds of sugar, so many eggs, and spice to your taste – the eggs to be beaten so and so, the whole mixed so and so, and baked so many minutes,' &c. &c. And thus with great care and industry they collect and write down, in a book which they keep for the purpose, all the recipes they can get hold of, for making every kind of cake and pastry used in society. And when they are preparing for company, they rarely if ever order Dinah or any other domestic to make their nice cake. They do not regard it as a menial office, but as a highly genteel employment; and their great desire to have their cake and pastry as good as it can be made, prompts them to undertake the manufacture of it themselves. And during this operation, the scales, the measures, the clock or watch, all are brought into requisition; the Recipe Book is placed upon the table before them, and carefully consulted; and everything is done with the utmost precision, and exactitude, and vigilance. And if the young lady feels any misgiving as to her own judgment, or taste, or experience, she earnestly inquires of Ma, of some one else who she thinks is capable of giving her advice in so important a matter.

If in the midst of this employment some one knocks or rings at the door, and a young gentleman is announced, she is not at all embarrassed, but perhaps hastens to the parlor with her delicate hands covered with dough, and with an air of complacency and self-satisfaction, says – 'Good morning, Frank – how do you do? I am just engaged in making some cake – I hope you will excuse me for a few moments.' All this shows that she regards the quality of her cake as of very great importance, and considers it not only perfectly respectable but highly *genteel*, for a young lady to be employed in making cake. But in regard to bread and breadmaking, everything is very different; there is none of this early curiosity to learn how to make good bread. Young ladies do not on every occasion when they find excellent bread, carefully and minutely inquire how it was made, baked, &c., and write down the recipe; but when a batch of bread is to be made for the family, they either leave it for Mother or some domestic to make, or go about it themselves as some irksome and disreputable piece of drudgery; and consequently they turn the task off their hands with as much despatch and as little trouble as possible. If all things happen to be as they should be, it is well; if not, they must answer for the present. If the yeast happens to be lively and sweet, very lucky. If otherwise, still it must be used. If the dough rises well and is got into the oven before it becomes sour, very fortunate; if not, why, 'nobody can avoid mistakes – and bread will sometimes be poor in spite of the greatest care;' – and if a batch of miserable bread is the result of such an operation, then all that remains to be done is to eat it up as soon as possible, and hope for better the next time.

If Frank or Charles or Edward should call while the young lady is engaged in making bread, she is perhaps quite disconcerted, and would not for the world have him know what she is doing; she sends word to him, either that she is out, or that she is particularly engaged, and begs he will excuse her; or if by any means she happens unexpectedly to be caught at her employment, she is greatly embarrassed, and makes the best apology she can for being engaged in such menial services.

As a matter of course, while such are the views and feelings entertained on this subject, and while such is the manner in which this duty is performed, it will ever be a mere accident if good bread is made; and a mere accident if such girls ever become good breadmakers when they are wives and mothers.

But if parents, and especially mothers, could view this matter in its true light, how differently would they educate their children. They would then feel that, grateful as it is to a mother's heart to see her daughters highly refined and elegantly accomplished, and able to 'make the instrument discourse most eloquent music,' and to transfer living nature, with all its truth and beauty and sublimity, to the canvass, still the art of breadmaking, when considered in all its relations and intimate connections with human health, and prosperity, and virtue, and happiness, and with reference to the natural responsibilities and duties of woman, is actually one of the highest and noblest accomplishments that can adorn the female character. And then, too, would they consider it of exceedingly great importance, that their daughters should possess this accomplishment, even though they may never be in circumstances which will require the exercise of it.

Some eight or nine years since, I spent several months in the delightful village of Belvidere, on the banks of the Delaware, in Pennsylvania. While there, I enjoyed for a number of weeks the kind hospitality of S— S—, Esq., a lawyer, and a gentleman of great moral excellence. Mrs S. was born and brought up, I believe, in Philadelphia. Her father was a man of wealth, and she was the only daughter, and – almost as a matter of course – was indulged in all that she desired. But there were so many of the elements of a good wife and mother in her natural composition, that as soon as she entered into those interesting and important relations, she began to devote herself to the duties of them with a sincerity and conscientiousness which could not fail of success. Surrounded as she was with wealth and every comfort and convenience of life, and all of its luxuries that she desired, still she was industrious in her habits, and vigilantly attentive to all the concerns of her household. She usually kept three female domestics, who, by her kind maternal deportment towards them, were warmly attached to her. She had no difficulty in procuring nor in keeping help, because she always treated them in such a manner that they loved to stay with her; and she took much pains to qualify them for the proper discharge of their duties. They evidently loved her, and were sincerely desirous of performing all their services in such a manner as would be pleasing to her. Yet with all these advantages to justify her leaving such a duty to her domestics, Mrs S. invariably made the family bread with her own hands. Regularly as the baking day came, she went into her kitchen and took her stand beside the bread trough, and mixed and kneaded the dough, and put it in its proper place for rising, and, in due time, moulded it into the loaf and baked it.

Do you always make your bread, madam? I inquired one day, as she returned from the performance of that task. 'Invariably,' she replied: 'that is a duty I trust no other person to do for me.'

But cannot your domestics make good bread? I asked. 'I have excellent domestics,' answered Mrs S., 'and they can, perhaps, make as good bread as I can; for they have been with me several years, and I have taken pains to learn them how to do my work; and they are exceedingly faithful and affectionate, and are always willing to do all they can to please me; but they cannot feel for my husband and my children as I do, and therefore they cannot feel that interest which I do, in always having such bread as my husband and my children will love and enjoy. Besides, if it were certain their care and vigilance and success in breadmaking would be always equal to mine, yet it is wholly uncertain how long they will remain with me. Various circumstances may take place, which may cause them to leave me, and bring me into dependence upon those who know not how to make good bread; and therefore I choose to keep my own hand in. But, apart from all other considerations, there is a pleasure resulting from the performance of this duty, which richly rewards me for all the labor of it. When my bread is made and brought upon the table, and I see my husband and children eat it and enjoy it, and hear them speak of its excellence, it affords me much satisfaction, and I am glad to know that I have contributed so much to their health and happiness; for, while my bread is so good that they prefer it to anything else upon the table, there is little danger of their indulging, to any injurious extent, in those articles of food which are less favorable to their health.'

I need not say that this lady invariably had excellent bread upon her table. But instances of this kind are, I regret to say, extremely rare, even in Christian communities; and therefore when such cases are known, they ought to be held up as most noble examples of female virtue, and receive such high commendations as their intrinsic merit deserves, and such as will be calculated to beget in the minds of others an exalted sense of the dignity and importance of such duties, and prompt every wife and mother to the intelligent and affectionate performance of them.

For it should ever be remembered that, though our children, while they depend on us for protection, are also properly the subjects of our government, yet as soon as they are capable of appreciating our authority and our influence, they are, like ourselves, moral agents, and ought, in all respects, to be governed and nurtured as such; and therefore it is not enough that we can give them such bread as we think best for them, and *compel* them to eat it; but the grand point at which the mother should always aim, in this matter, is, to place before her children such bread as is the very best for them, and at the same time, to make it the most agreeable to them, and thereby make their duty and their enjoyment perfectly coincide.

Let no one therefore say she cannot always have good bread, until she can truly affirm that she has fairly made the experiment; that she has, in view of all its relations and hearings, accurately estimated the importance of the quality of her bread in regard to the welfare of her household, and, with a proper sense of her responsibilities as a wife and mother, has *at all times* felt that interest and exercised that care and attention which so important a duty demands, and without which it must ever be a mere accident whether her bread is good or bad.

They that will have good bread, not only for a single time, but uniformly, must make the quality of their bread of sufficient importance, in their estimation and feelings, to secure the requisite attention to the means by which alone such an end can be made certain. They must not suffer themselves, through carelessness, to get entirely out of bread unexpectedly, and thus be obliged, without due preparation, to make up a batch of such materials as they may happen to have at hand, and bake it in haste, and hurry it to the table. But they must exercise providence and foresight: they must know, beforehand, when their supply of bread will probably be out, and when they will need to make another batch; and they must see beforehand that measures are taken to secure a proper supply of all the requisite materials – see that they are furnished with good meal or flour; and they must be sure to have the best of yeast or leaven, when they need it – and when the time comes for them to make their bread, if by any means the yeast should not be good, let them throw it away and make good, before they proceed to make their bread; for it is infinitely better that the family should even do without bread one day, and eat roasted potatoes, than that they should eat poor bread three or four days; and if, from any cause, the bread should be poor, it is incomparably better to throw it away, than to set it upon the table, to disgust the whole family with bread, and drive them to make most of their meal on something else.

If a lady can ever find a good excuse for having poor bread, she certainly can find none, except perhaps extreme poverty, for setting her poor bread on the table the second time. Yet, too generally, women seem to think that, as a matter of course, if they, by carelessness or any other means, have been so unlucky as to make a batch of poor bread, their family and friends must share their misfortune, and help them eat it up; and, by this means, many a child has had its health seriously impaired, and its constitution injured, and perhaps its moral character ruined – by being driven, in early life, into pernicious dietetic habits.

It was observed many years ago, by one of the most eminent and extensive practitioners in New England, that, during a practice of medicine for thirty years, he had always remarked that, in those families where the children were most afflicted with worms, he invariably found poor bread; and that, as a general fact, the converse of this was true; that is, in those families where they uniformly had heavy, sour, ill-baked bread, he generally found that the children were afflicted with worms.

A careful and extensive observation for a few years, would convince every intelligent mind that there is a far more intimate relation between the quality of the bread and the moral character of a family, than is generally supposed.

'Keep that man at least ten paces from you, who eats no bread with his dinner,' said Lavater, in his *Aphorisms on Man*. This notion appears to be purely whimsical at first glance;

but Lavater was a shrewd observer, and seldom erred in the moral inferences which he drew from the voluntary habits of mankind; and depend upon it, a serious contemplation of this apparent whim discloses a deeper philosophy than is at first perceived upon the surface.

Whatever may be the cause which turns our children and ourselves away from the dish of bread, and establishes an habitual disregard for it, the effect, though not perhaps in every individual instance, yet, as a general fact, is certainly, in some degree, unfavorable to the physical, and intellectual, and moral, and religious, and social, and civil and political interests of man.

Of all the artificially prepared articles of food which come upon our table, therefore, bread should be that one which, as a general fact, is uniformly preferred by our children and our household, that one, the absence of which they would notice soonest, and feel the most, that one which – however they may enjoy for a time the little varieties set before them – they would be most unwilling to dispense with – and which, if they were driven to the necessity, they would prefer to any other dish, as a single article of subsistence.

To effect this state of things, it is obvious that the quality of the bread must be uniformly excellent; and to secure this, I say again, there must be a judgment, an experience, a skill, a care, a vigilance, which can only spring from the sincere affections of a devoted wife and mother, who accurately perceives and duly appreciates the importance of these things, and, in the lively exercise of a pure and delicate moral sense, feels deeply her responsibilities, and is prompted to the performance of her duties.

Would to God that this were all true of every wife and mother in our country – in the world! – that the true relations, and interests, and responsibilities of life were understood and felt by every human being, and all the duties of life properly and faithfully performed!

Varieties of Bread

Rye bread. Indian meal bread. Use of sour milk, or butter-milk. Acids. Family grinding.

I have thus far spoken almost entirely of wheaten bread, because I consider that the most wholesome kind of bread for ordinary use – for 'daily bread'. When bread is made of superfine flour, the same general rules should be observed.

Rice, barley, oats, rye, Indian corn, and many other farinaceous products of the vegetable kingdom, may also be manufactured into bread, but none of them will make so good bread as wheat. Good rye, raised on a sandy soil, when cleansed and ground in the manner I have already described, and prepared in all respects according to the rules I have laid down, will make very excellent bread. Rye, coarsely ground, without bolting, and mixed with Indian meal, makes very wholesome bread, when it is well made. Good rye and Indian bread is far more wholesome for common or every-day use, than that made of superfine flour.

There are various ways of preparing Indian meal bread; and when such bread is well made, it is very wholesome – much more so, for every-day use, than superfine flour bread.

'In a memoir lately read before the French Academy,' says the Journal of Health, 'the author undertook to show that maize (Indian corn) is more conducive to health than any other grain; and, as a proof of this, the fact was adduced that, in one of the departments in which this grain was most abundantly and universally used, the inhabitants were remarkable for their health and vigor.'

One great drawback to the wholesomeness of Indian meal bread, however, is, that it is almost universally eaten hot, and too generally, pretty well oiled with butter, or some other kind of animal fat or oil. But Indian meal bread can be prepared in such a manner as to obviate these difficulties, and render it very wholesome.

Barley and oats may be manufactured into very wholesome bread; but they are little used for such purposes in this country.

Rice, peas, beans, potatoes, &c., may also, by mixing them with a portion of wheat or rye flour, be manufactured into bread; but, as I have already stated, there is no other kind of grain or farinaceous vegetable substance from which so good loaf bread can be made, as good wheat.

In making bread from Indian meal, and other kinds of farinaceous substances containing little or no gluten, yeast or leaven is rarely if ever used to make it light. More generally sour milk or butter-milk and saleratus or soda are used for this purpose; and they who do not well understand the principle upon which these substances make their bread light, often greatly impair their own success by their mismanagement.

It is, perhaps, most common for them to mix their sour milk or butter-milk and saleratus together, and wait till the effervescence is over, before they stir in their meal. But by this means they lose the greater part of the gas or air by which their dough should be made light.

The true way is, to take their sour milk or butter-milk, and stir meal into it till a thin batter is formed, and then dissolve their saleratus or soda, and stir that quickly and thoroughly into the batter, and then hastily add meal till the batter or dough is brought into the consistency desired.

If, instead of sour milk or butter-milk, a solution of muriatic or tartaric acid is used, the bread will be equally light. In this case, the batter should be first made with a solution of saleratus or soda, and then the solution of acid should be stirred in as above described. Batter cakes are made in this manner very light and very promptly. When from any cause batter or dough mixed with yeast fails to rise according to expectations, the thorough mixing in, first the solution of muriatic or tartaric acid, and then the solution of saleratus or soda, will, in a few minutes, make the whole mass very light; but such cakes and bread are not so sweet and savory as those raised with good sweet yeast.

I have said that recently ground meal makes far sweeter and richer bread, than that which has been ground a considerable time; but as it is not convenient for many families to send to a mill as often as they would like to have fresh meal, they are obliged generally to use staler meal or flour than they would choose. Yet every family might easily be furnished with a modern patent hand-mill, constructed after the plan of a coffee mill, with which they could at all times, with great ease, grind their wheat, and rice, and corn, as they want it, for bread and other purposes. With these mills they can grind their stuff as finely or coarsely as they wish, for bread or hominy, and always have it very fresh and sweet.

A Flemish ink drawing detailing the breadmaking process, dating from the mid-1200s. (The Getty Museum)

Here a Syrian peasant is seen making bread in the Holy Land, *c.* 1890.
(Library of Congress)

Women bake bread outdoors in Caucasus, Georgia, *c.* 1880–1900. (Library of Congress)

Pictured here in New Mexico, 1907, two Pueblo Indian women bake bread in their oven. (Library of Congress)

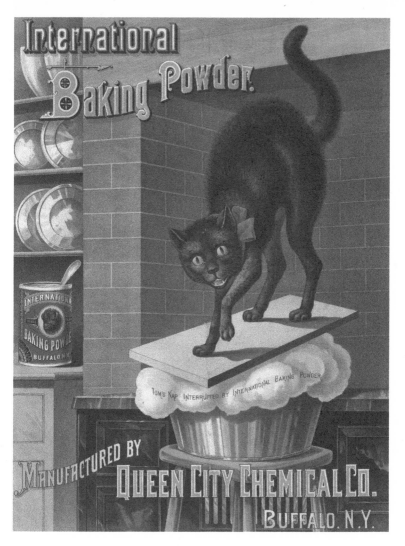

An advertisement for 'International Baking Powder' by the Queen City
Chemical Co., New York, dating back to 1885. (Library of Congress)

'Mother's bread – pure as mother made it'. An advertisement for the J.A. Dahn & Son baking company, *c*. 1900, plays on domestic ideals to sell its bread. (Library of Congress)

In contrast, we have a glimpse at the reality of public bakeries in the US. In the early twentieth century, fifteen-year-old Vincenzo Messina and his eleven-year-old brother, Angelo, work the night shift at a bakery in Massachusetts. (Library of Congress)

Another view from a bakery in New York, *c.* 1920. (Library of Congress)

An interesting look at military life in a camp in France during the First World War – the men are making bread to feed the British Army. (Library of Congress)

A view of a young woman removing bread in an advertisement for ovens made by the Born Range Co., dated 1909. (Library of Congress)

The Modern Practical Bread Baker

Robert Wells

Preface

Probably there are few callings that can claim an older or more respectable origin than that of the baking trade, and nothing marks the progress of the world's cuisine more clearly than the difference that exists between ancient and modern breadmaking. It is interesting to note the change. The earliest method was to soak the grain in water and to dry it by natural or artificial heat, after having subjected it to pressure. The next advance was to pound or bray the grains in a mortar, or between stones; hence the word bread – *brayed*.

The oat-cakes of Scotland are prepared from grains that have been ground somewhat more thoroughly, and mixed with salt and water, kneaded and rolled out thin, and cooked before a good fire or on an iron girdle hung above the fire. Scones and pea meal bannocks are made in the same way. The Passover cakes of the Israelites are similarly prepared. The Southern hoe cake does not differ materially from the above varieties, which are all called unleavened, no leaven being used in their manufacture. Leaven is literally that which is applied internally to raise the bread, and it was first used by the Egyptians – presumably in the time of Moses. From the Egyptians it spread to the Greeks, then to the Romans, and from them to all parts of the world.

The baking industry (or the baking trade, as it is commonly called) has a deeper and fuller interest to mankind than any of its offshoots – pastry, confectionery, etc., as the one is a necessity and the others only luxuries. The staff of life, let it be made by man or woman, requires to be properly manipulated. This is of the most paramount interest, and assuredly goes to at once build up the wealth and stamina of a nation.

Flour

Flour being one of the primary substances used in the manufacture of bread, and its good or bad qualities having everything to do with the bread baker's failure or success, I propose to treat of it in the first instance, and make it, as it were, my starting-point or foundation on which to raise the structure of my experiences.

In the buying of flour a modern baker should be a thorough expert. He should be capable of using his own practical judgment; judgment, too, of no mean order, but based on past experience. No man should buy a hundred sacks of flour at less than market value without first ascertaining its quality and condition. To buy cheaply is a good point, but to buy well is a better. Hr. Thoms, of Alyth, and Professor Jago have each invented an apparatus for testing flour, both of which are very easily understood and are of considerable value to the trade. Of course, the surest way of testing flour is by setting a sponge and baking a small quantity of bread from it; but the baker or buyer may form a pretty accurate idea of its quality by pressing a portion of the flour between the thumb and forefinger, and at the same time rubbing it gently in the hand for the purpose of making a level surface on the flour. If the flour feels loose and lively in the hand it may be supposed to be of good quality; but if it feels dead, damp, or clammy it is decidedly bad. Or take a watch with a smooth back and press it firmly upon the flour; by this means its colour may be ascertained by observing the pressed or smooth surface. If the flour be fine and white it may be considered good so far as colour goes; if brown, it shows that it is either made from inferior wheat or has been coarsely dressed. Brown flour, however, may be of good quality, and fine white flour may not; and bakers ought not to forget that flour should be kept a short time before being made into bread.

Flour's colour and appearance have been the most important factors in producing the recent revolutions in milling methods. Even those millers who believed that stone-milled flour made sweeter and better flavoured bread have gradually adopted roller-milled flour in its place. The reason of this is that bread made from roller-milled flour has a richer and better appearance.

Anyone watching the transactions between buyers and sellers at any of our leading corn markets will notice that one of the most frequent tests made is to place flours side by side and smooth their surfaces with a spatula, in order to show the relative qualities of colour. This test is familiar to nearly all millers and bakers, for it is doubtful whether there is a more fruitful source of dispute between them than colour. A parcel of flour is, perhaps, bought for forward delivery, and is taken from the miller in instalments. Most likely the first instalment is in every way equal to the sample from which the purchase was made, but after a while, as successive lots come in, differences are observed between the first and last received. As time goes on, the miller perhaps alters his mixture, and finds considerable difficulty in keeping his flour at a constant standard of colour. This is a difficulty everywhere, even when the same variety of wheat is being used. The sole remedy is close care and watchfulness.

In the larger mills samples of flour are tested and examined several times a day for colour and other properties. In order to explain discrepancies between bulk and sample, the theory of bleaching is commonly resorted to. That is to say, the sample apparently grows whiter by keeping, and thus presents a different appearance from the bulk. It is, however, more than doubtful whether this is a sufficient explanation in the majority of instances where a dispute has arisen on this matter of colour.

CHEMICAL EXAMINATION OF FLOUR

This is really not millers' work, nor that of the merchant, but should be done by well-educated scientific chemists, as is commonly the case in France, where science and industry go hand in hand and mutually aid each other. By an examination so conducted, the limits of water, starch, gluten, and ashes are determined. The water contents of flour are easily ascertained by drying out a small quantity in an air-bath, at a temperature of 110° or 120°C. The driest flour contains 6 per cent of water, while in some instances it will be found to contain as much as 25 per cent. The properties of starch and gluten are determined by separating one from the other. Tie the flour up in a small linen bag and knead it under water until the gluten has formed into a mass, which, if the flour is of poor quality, it will not do for a long time. In the water in which the flour is thus kneaded the starch will be found, and will very shortly settle at the bottom. Cerealin and casein, both nourishing nitrogenous substances, are entirely lost in the examination, as they quickly dissolve. The secured gluten and the settled starch are weighed together; thus the quantities are ascertained. For the determination of gluten, MM. Bolin and Robins, of Paris, have invented an ingenious instrument called an aleurometer, by which a baking process is gone through and the quantity found with ease. The ashes are determined by burning a certain quantity, which is afterwards weighed, and may reach from 1.5 to 2.2 per cent; if more than this, adulteration by mineral substances is to be suspected, and must be traced by chemical analysis.

But there are also practical tests which are of equal importance to the miller and baker, especially chemicals for improving the general appearance.

Experienced men are, of course, the most accurate judges of the feel, colour, and general appearance of good flours, but it not infrequently happens that even they are compelled to use a microscope. The principal defect in flour, and one difficult of detection, is that which causes the flowing of the dough when it does not rise, but instead spreads itself on the sides. This may be attributed to the presence of wild garlic, the quality of the land on which the wheat grew, etc. Herr Oser, of Krems, in 'Niedercesterrich,' suggests an original expedient to test the quality of flour, viz.: – Take 16 grammes of flour from every exhibitor, and knead these singly in eight grammes of water. The best flour will give the stiffest dough.

So far as baking-flour is concerned, it should not be too fine, for fine flour bakes harder than coarse flour, being much less vaporous. Good flour should be of a yellowish colour, and much practical experience is needed for proper discrimination between the superior and inferior grades.

To test flour in order to ascertain the admixture of rye flour, potato flour, etc., the Pekar flour-tester is the most reliable. It is patented, and can only be used in the mill on payment of a yearly royalty of 1 kroner per 109 kilogrammes. Microscopical examinations also show adulterations, and for this test a magnifying power of 800 to 400 diameters is necessary. The particles of rye flour are larger than those of wheat or barley flour, but the difference in size is not very great. This examination is, therefore, not reliable, more especially as by it quality merely, not quantity, can be ascertained. It is much more easy to detect the addition of oats, millet, rice, or maize, as the starch particles of these are much more apparent, the maize starch being largest of all, and therefore most easily observed. The outer husk of millet flour is ground largely along with it. Rice flour is entirely free from husks or shells, because these shell with the gluten husk, and therefore the quantity of gluten is very small; the starch kernels are angular, and the colour of the flour is a beautiful white. Oat flour contains bran, which cannot altogether be removed. In many places oats are not ground to flour.

Wheat flour is adulterated by being mixed with rye, barley, or rice flour – especially with the latter.

Flour adulterated with bean or pea flour is known by the elliptical shape of the starch particles of the latter. Adulteration by mineral matter is immediately detected by the microscope, presenting as it does the appearance of a grey, formless mass. From practical experience I have found that reliable brands of Hungarian flour are 'E.O.P', 'Concordia,' and 'P.W.M.'.

SPICED FLOUR

Of late years our workshops have been pretty well inundated
with what millers term 'spiced flour'. This does not seem to be
confined to any one district, as I have had the misfortune to
work it in Carlisle and in Scarborough. It must be a source of
great loss to both miller and baker, and I have known more
than one business seriously affected by the occasional use of it.
From inquiry made, I find it is caused by a parasite, peculiar
to California, that grows in the germs of wheat, but cannot
be discovered by the naked eye. The flour milled from this
particular wheat has, when baked, a peculiar spicy taste and
flavour which is anything but agreeable.

On Yeasts and Barms

As I consider flour the primary substance in the manipulation of bread, so I think it will not be out of order to place yeast next, as playing a good secondary part. The many varieties of yeasts now before the public, whether used privately or advertised by wholesale merchants, are legion. Were we to believe all the references given for, and the results said to be obtained by, the various so-called yeasts, we should be tempted to think that at last the baking community had reached that El Dorado which they have so long striven to attain. But if we are induced to try one of these fancy-named brands, we invariably find it to be but an old one newly named, and sent forth again to make more full an already well-stocked market, with an 'F.I.C.' attached to it, to 'raise' it in the estimation of the public.

That there are good and inferior brands every practical baker will admit who has had anything to do with the working of compressed yeasts; but I believe that the good brands outweigh the inferior ones. I could mention half-a-dozen brands that have all the qualities a modern baker could desire; and in the following chapter I will try and show the reader what a really good yeast should be, in as plain language as the subject I am treating of will allow. And as this work is written for the special use of journeymen bakers, I am vain enough to hope that it may assist in the removal of some of the stumbling-blocks that beset their way, and may prove a benefit to a few of my brothers in trade.

PARISIAN BARM

Let us take our first lesson on Parisian barm.

The baker should see that his barm tub is clean and dry before it is used. Put one gallon of water, heated to about 140°F, into a pan or earthen pot; weigh two pounds of crushed malt, and place it in the water. Cover the mixture up and let the malt steep for about three hours. One hour before you intend to make your barm – i.e. after the malt has been steeping two hours – put a large pan containing three gallons of water upon the fire. When this boils add two ounces of good, fresh hops; this must be boiled for twenty minutes. While the hop-water is boiling, strain the malt water into the barm tub through a hair sieve, squeezing each lot of malt in your hands so thoroughly as to leave no water or juice in it. (The sieve should be placed over the tub, resting on sticks lying across its top). After this add to the malt water as much flour as can be stirred in it, using the barm stick to stir with. Next put the boiling hop water through a sieve over the malt and flour water, and stir well. The baker must be very expeditious in scalding his malt water and flour, as one of the necessary points in the manufacture of this barm is to ensure its being thoroughly scalded. Assistance is required in the removal of the pot or pan from the fire, and in putting the liquid into the tub, while the operator stands with the barm stick ready in his hand, and commences to stir the ingredients as soon as may be, so that the flour be thoroughly scalded. Too strong a flour scalds badly; therefore the baker should note what flour answers best, and stick to it.

Instead of putting the hops direct into the water, many bakers place them inside a small linen bag made for the purpose. In this way they require half-an-hour to boil; the bag should be pressed and squeezed against the pan sides before it is taken out. The operator then throws the boiling hop water upon the malt water and flour, and stirs as before.

Supposing the time to be five o'clock in the afternoon, the tub, covered with a sack or two to prevent the mass from growing too cold, is put aside till next morning, when it should be stirred with the hand, the thick or jellied parts that adhere to the sides being all thoroughly mixed. See that the liquid (it cannot yet be termed barm) is not too hot for setting away; the right heat is about 85°. Add half a gallon of barm, previously made, and stir well; then put the liquid aside in a nice temperature to work itself ready. This should take not more than eight or ten hours, though much depends on the heat of the surrounding atmosphere. When about ready you will see a thin froth start generally at one side of the tub and gradually work over to the other side, though I have seen it start to spread from the middle. By following this method, circumstances being favourable, you cannot fail to have good Parisian barm.

Barm of this nature has a dull, worked-out, greasy appearance, with little or no life in it. Where the trade is small, and will only allow of the barm being made twice a week, I should advise the baker to procure three or four earthen pots, and when the barm is ready, divide what is required for each day into these pots, along with the store of barm required to start the next making. In doing this he will, in great measure, protect himself against harbouring impure ferments. But Parisian barm should, if possible, be made every day.

ON 'BRINGING AWAY' PARISIAN BARM WITHOUT ANY PREVIOUSLY MADE BARM BEING MIXED WITH THE FRESHLY MADE LIQUID

This can with skilful hands be easily done, but I should not advise the amateur to adopt this method until he has thoroughly mastered the difficulties presented by fermentation. In places where it is done – and there are such places – a recess, sufficiently large to hold a small pot of the size of about a half-gallon tin, is built in the front of the oven. Proceed as follows:–

After your liquid has been scalded and made, take three pints of it and place it in the above-mentioned recess. Keep it at a fixed temperature, and stir it up three or four times a day. After the first day add four ounces of moist cane sugar, and continue stirring occasionally till you see it beginning to ferment. Then let it ferment till ready; it should again be stirred and kept in a warm atmosphere till the fermenting process is completed.

As I said before, a skilful Parisian barm-maker can do it, but it should not be attempted by an amateur, as both knowledge and skill are required to bring it away.

VIRGIN BARM

Virgin barm, or bastard barm, as it is sometimes called, is made in somewhat the same way as Parisian barm, with the exception that there is neither malt nor hops used. It is nothing more than scalded flour; but I have seen barm of this kind make splendid bread. It should be made frequently, as it is apt to weaken if not kept up with a good store of Parisian barm – i.e., the three quarts of barm given to it to cause fermentation or to make it work. The mode of manufacture is entirely the same as that required in making Parisian barm, and it has this in its favour – it is easily made, and is cheap.

Boil three gallons of water in a pan, and sift what flour you think will be required, and put it in a tub; pour the boiling water upon it, during which it should be well stirred, and will, if properly scalded, grow thick during the process. Some bakers only take two gallons for the first scald, taking the remaining gallon for a second scalding. The scalding must be thorough, or it is useless. When the heat is down to about 86°, start it with three quarts of previously made barm. This is really a capital barm, but, like others, requires attention.

MALT AND HOP BARM

or composition barm, as it is in some places called, is another good barm; there is no mystery or difficulty in connection with its manufacture.

Procure a large pan, and put into it three gallons of water. Sift through a fine sieve two pounds of crushed malt, and put what remains in the sieve into the water in the pan, along with two ounces of good fresh hops. Either boil this for an hour, or put it into the oven the last thing at night, and remove it the first thing next morning. Strain it through a fine sieve when cold enough for use, squeezing it well with the hand till no moisture remains in the malt and hops. Set the liquid apart till it is thoroughly cold; the temperature may be 68° or 70°F. The sifted malt, together with a pint of previously made malt and hop barm, is now to be mixed with the liquid to start it to work (or set away).

This barm must be cool when worked, and in working it should come up with a nice frothy cauliflower head. I have made this barm set away with an ounce of German yeast with good results; but the other is preferable.

This barm is best adapted for potato fermentation. I have tested it, in setting a ferment – quite cold – two days before using it, with only a pint and a half of barm to eighteen stone of flour, and it produced a loaf that was, in flavour, colour and texture, all that a practical man could desire.

STORE

Store is a flour barm that was, some twenty-four years ago, in general use in Scotland (at least in the south); but now, unless by some of the very old school, it is seldom used, Parisian and virgin barm being easier to make and having better keeping qualities. Still, when this barm was all right, I have seen very good bread made from it, but I never liked its flavour. It was mostly used for potato ferments. I have seen tub after tub of it thrown away, especially when there was an atmospheric change.

Boil three gallons of water, into which (in a bag made for the purpose) put four ounces of good hops. After half-an-hour's boiling, squeeze the bag against the sides of the pan, to get rid of all juice from the hops. The store-stick should be in the tub with the quantity of flour required, which quantity a baker can only know by experience; then take one half of the boiling water from the fire, and give the mixture the first scalding. Stir till you can stir no longer, which will soon be, as the store has to be as thick as ordinary batch dough; when the first scald is completed, hand your store-stick to an assistant and let him have a try. The remainder of the boiling hop water may now be taken; see that a proper scald is effected, for on this the quality of the store depends. The store should now be about the size of pie dough; when properly scalded, put it away, as for other barms, covered with a sack, till nearly cold; then add half a gallon of previously prepared store, to set away. Or, by keeping the batter at a regular heat, this barm can be brought away by itself; also by stirring it up in the tub till fermentation ensues. Then let it work itself ready, when it should rise in the tub about two inches, and drop the same distance.

This is a most difficult barm to make, as it requires a very skilful man, and will soon go sour if the tubs are not properly scalded and cleansed. I have seen a tub of this store spoiled by a single accidental knock during the early stages of fermentation.

AMERICAN PATENT YEAST

Take half a pound of hops and two pailfuls of water; mix and boil till the liquid is reduced one half; strain the decoction into a tub, and when lukewarm add half a peck of malt. In the meantime put the drained-off hops again into two pailfuls of water and boil as before, till the liquid is reduced one half; then strain the hot liquid into a tub. (The heat will not injuriously affect malt previously mixed with tepid water.) When the liquid has cooled to about 85°F, strain off the malt and add to the liquid two quarts of patent yeast of a previous making. This should make five gallons of good yeast, which will be ready for use the day after it is made. It takes about eight hours to make, and gives very little trouble to the baker.

BREWER'S BARM

has fallen greatly into disuse, and Parisian barm, patent barm, virgin barm and compressed yeast have taken the lead. Brewers' barm requires to be worked with a potato ferment, and potato ferments I consider to be things of the past. They have answered their purpose, I dare say, very well; but this is another instance of the 'survival of the fittest.' Potato ferments must give way to better and more modern methods. These ferments are mostly used in Scotland and in some parts of London. It is, indeed, strange that two of our largest bread-producing centres should be the last to give up the old, mediaeval style of doing things. Old customs die hard; still, I have seen potato ferments of service when used in weak or soft flour. But flour ferments, quarter sponges, half sponges, and full sponges are the order of the day. I never took very kindly to brewers' barm, as I fancied it left a peculiar taste in the bread. In Liverpool and its vicinity, brewers' barm is in common use, and it has this peculiarity, that a certain amount of salt is used with the ferment while it is working.

GERMAN YEAST

German yeasts – their name is legion – have entirely revolutionised the baking trade – at any rate, on this side of the border. Our trade is in this respect in no way different from others. New appliances, ingenious instruments, and complicated machinery, in connection with trades and handicrafts, have constantly arisen, and are continuing to increase, some undoubtedly being great improvements and supplying urgent needs, others being of a less beneficial character. But be that as it may, the introduction of German yeast has been a great and acknowledged boon to the baking trade.

The name German yeast includes, to a baker's mind, all kinds of compressed yeast, English, Scotch, French or German.

Good brands come from Germany, yeast that the manufacturers may well be proud of. But there are an equal number of inferior brands, which are generally used for retail purposes, and sold to housewives and people out of the trade. When they get inferior brands of yeast to work, the flour is usually blamed; they do not take into consideration their own incapacity, or the quality of the yeast they are using.

SCOTCH YEAST

is made in some of the breweries in the north of Scotland. Some twelve years ago I used this kind of yeast, but at that time did not like it – it was too weak and feeble, having very small powers of fermentation about it. The Scotch manufacturers have, however, very much improved their methods of making yeast since then, and are now producing an article which is taking a high stand in the market.

FRENCH YEAST

Some really good brands of yeast come from France. But it would be unfair to specify any; France keeps well abreast with every other country in manufacturing this particular article.

ENGLISH COMPRESSED YEAST

There is a particular brand of compressed yeast manufactured in England that will more than hold its own for quality and price with any of those above referred to. I have used it daily for twelve months, and can testify to its merits. It has good strength and flavour, and is good in every way – more especially when the reasonableness of its price is taken into consideration. (The increased daily demand for the best brands of English compressed yeast conclusively proves my assertion. I would invite all who use foreign yeasts to compare the above yeasts with the best French, German and Danish productions, and I have no doubt as to the result. Why send money out of the country when an article of superior quality, and at a cheaper price, can be bought at your doors? Besides, you have the satisfaction of knowing that you are helping to encourage home industries.)

COMPRESSED YEASTS WHEN STALE AND UNFIT FOR USE

Now that the greater part of the bread made in the United Kingdom is fermented with compressed yeasts, a short dissertation on the appearance of yeast when seen in the above-named undesirable condition will, I think, be of use to the practical baker. Continental yeasts, when seen in this state, are, as a rule, dark, soft, and clammy; the odour becomes loathsome and disagreeable, and there is none of that pleasant, fresh, barmy smell, so much admired by those bakers who use it. The softening of yeasts of this class, and their bad appearance, are said to be due to incipient germination, caused by excessive heat and moisture. I may likewise add that the same disagreeable results may be brought about by rough usage, such as carelessly throwing the yeast about, etc., which causes it to germinate and feed upon its own substance, thereby weakening its properties and in a very short time rendering it unfit for any practical use.

Compressed yeasts made in Britain, when bad or stale, present quite a different appearance. I may say that I have studied the appearance and practical results of these in their various stages of decomposition for a number of years, and have found that the British-made yeasts, when in this state, become very dry; the temperature of the yeast is also high, and it is warm to the touch. The colour becomes white, and, when the weakening process goes on apace, instead of softening like continental yeasts when passing from the healthy to the unhealthy stages, it becomes dry and crumbly, and entirely unfit for use.

If compressed yeast is kept in the vicinity of salt, the action of the atmosphere on this commodity will render the yeast soft, and in a short time it will become useless. To prove this, place a small piece of fresh yeast amongst a little salt, when it will soon begin to liquefy. Care must therefore be taken, and arrangement made to keep yeast in as pure an atmosphere as the conditions of the bakery will permit.

My motive in writing this short article on the appearance of bad yeasts in their various stages of deterioration, is to put the baker on his guard, and to warn him against using them in too debilitated a condition. Recently I saw it stated in one of our trade journals that a practical man has no guide to aid him in this dilemma, save his judgment and experience of smell and taste; likewise, that there are no rough-and-ready tests that have any degree of reliability. Well, if this be true, our modern practical bread baker is in a very precarious, unenviable position. No better, simpler, or surer test could a workman desire, surely, than that given in a former work of mine, *The Bread and Biscuit Baker*, on page 11. So far as my own experience goes, and that of those who have wisely adopted the test, I have never known it to fail.

For the benefit of those who have not read that work, I here repeat the description of the test:–

Procure a clean cup or tumbler; half fill it with warm water, temperature 100°; place an ounce of lump sugar in the water, and, when this has dissolved, add one ounce of the suspected yeast. The yeast will first sink to the bottom; if in a workable state it will rise to the top in two minutes. If a much longer time is required for rising, dependence should not be placed upon its fermenting qualities. The strength of the yeast you are testing is shown entirely by the time it takes to rise to the top of the water.

HOW TO KEEP YEAST PURE

In the year 1080, yeast was found to contain organic matter; but scientists did not give it attention till M. Pasteur undertook the study of it. It is from him that we have obtained our chief knowledge of ferments, and one of the most useful discoveries of scientific chemistry is the knowledge how to keep yeast pure.

Where there is difficulty in keeping yeast pure, one of M. Pasteur's suggestions may perhaps be valuable: it is especially applicable during warm weather. The yeast, he suggests, should be grown in sweetened water, in successive growths, a small percentage of tartaric acid being added; also by growing it in wort, adding a few drops of phonel. It requires care and attention, and is a very valuable method in warm climates and weathers.

LEAVEN

is nothing more nor less than flour and water, stirred together and kept in a warm place until fermentation commences. Every time the baker makes bread, a certain quantity should be kept back in an earthen pot for the next sponge.

The use of leaven is supposed to have originated in Egypt. It is very seldom used in this country now, although in some parts of Cumberland it occurs in the manufacture of a particular kind of brown bread. In some European countries where yeast is not easily obtained leaven is used. Sailors use it on long voyages. But, like most things where fermentation is concerned, care and cleanliness must be observed. But let leaven be ever so well manufactured, the bread made from it has always a rank, sour taste, and is not to be compared with yeast-made bread.

The degrees of heat given in the preceding pages for starting barms to work, etc., are for use in winter. Less heat will suffice in summer. The temperature of the bakehouse will likewise have to be taken into consideration. This also applies to sponging.

SALT

Salt, or chloride of sodium, has more to do in checking fermentation and seasoning bread than most practical bakers will admit.

I have no doubt that when the practical baker studies chemistry, as in time the exigencies of his trade must force him to do, and he thoroughly understands the properties and constituent parts of this necessary – but nearly altogether neglected – substance, it will take a higher place in the estimation of practical men that it at present occupies. In fact, when conversing with men on the respective qualities of bread, salt is rarely mentioned.

Flour and yeast are, I confess, the main factors in bread making; but I really think that salt plays third part in producing the 'staff of life'.

Salt is obtained in various ways – as fossil or rock salt; from the boiling or evaporation of salt springs; and from the sea.

In a pure state it consists of 60 per cent, of chlorine, and 40 per cent, of sodium. Salt, with food, acts as a tonic, aids the digestive powers of the stomach, and assists in assimilating fatty substances. It is, therefore, an important article.

WATER

being a necessary element in bread manufacture, a few words must be said about it. I have noticed that bread made under the same conditions, and with the same brands of flour and yeast, varies so much in different districts, that I have been inclined to doubt the similarity of the ingredients. The only reason that I can assign for this difference of quality is that the chemical properties of the water employed are different; and a baker's practical experience will very soon tide him over this difficulty. Water taken from a boiler that is built on a chaffer or furnace should not be used for sponging, as it is liable to get too much boiled, by which it loses part of its chemical properties. Anyone can easily prove this by making tea with water that has boiled for half an hour or longer, and then with water that has just come to the boil. The flavour of the tea made from the latter will be far superior to that made from the former; and what applies to tea, correspondingly applies to bread.

Now, having introduced to the reader the various qualities of flour, yeast, salt, and water, let me blend them together as a whole in the endeavour to produce bread that will satisfy alike the palate of a pampered epicure, and the trained, scrutinising eye of a practical baker.

Fermentation

The meaning of the word 'fermentation' should be of great interest to the modern journeyman baker. But if the simple question as to its true meaning is put, out of every hundred answers how many will be correct?

Pasteur, the renowned chemist and physiologist, says:

> My most decided opinion on the nature of alcoholic fermentation is: the chemical act of fermentation is essentially a correlative phenomenon of a vital act beginning and ending with it. I think there is never any alcoholic fermentation without there being at the same time organisation, development, multiplication of globules, or the continued consecutive life of globules already formed.

The process has for its object either the manufacture of bread, or of an alcoholic product in a more or less concentrated form – both very similar in action during the earlier stages. It communicates with the growth and multiplication of the fermenting germs contained in the minute organisms floating in the air, and the inorganic constituents of the water; and all the changes are produced by heat.

Dr Ducleaux, of Paris, in his *Handbook on Fermentation*, says that:

The history of microbes can be reduced to an examination of the nutritive requirements, and of their means of satisfying them. It is there that the great difference between them and the higher animals is to be found. The latter are also formed of cells, individually nearly as small as those of ferments; but these cells, which possess various properties, and are bound up in various tissues, are naturally subjected, through the medium of the blood, the nerves, and the muscles, to a series of profound and complex actions, on which physiology will gradually throw light. The study of microbes is exempt from such complications. Here the cells are free and independent; their principal – I might say their only – occupation is that of feeding. The latter only depends on questions of alimentary matter, of temperature, of moisture, which we can easily master. The problem is, therefore, relatively speaking, an easy one. Let us study it carefully. We shall be rewarded by the discovery that its solution, once found, can be applied in a general manner, and will supply a key to the understanding of the nutrition of the higher animals.

This nutrition necessitates the presence of a certain number of different elements, which may be divided under four heads. Every cell contains nitrogenous organic matter, non-nitrogenous, and mineral matter, thus requiring for nutrition: (1) nitrogen, (2) carbohydrates, (3) minerals. Moreover, every cell breathes, thus needing (4) gaseous aliments.

I will begin with the last, and show what a fertile field of study it and the others open out.

At first it may be thought that yeast does not breathe, in the sense that we usually attach to the word, that is to say, that it does not require oxygen.

In order that a fresh fermentation may be produced, it has been shown that the brewer takes the seed from a former fermentation, where the liquid is saturated with carbonic acid and does not contain air. When once it is in the wort the yeast almost immediately produces carbonic acid, and is in an atmosphere where there is no oxygen. This has been taking place for centuries, and the yeast at present in use seems to have descended from that which the brewers in Egypt used 6,000 years ago, by a series of successive generations, and a process which must apparently have taken place in the absence of oxygen.

Dr Ducleaux continues to say that:

If a beetroot be put in carbonic acid, it will produce alcohol; cherries, plums, apples, any sweet fruit or sacchariferous plants treated similarly will still have the sugar they contain partly turned into alcohol and carbonic acid under these new conditions of life.

The only difference between these and yeast is that they are much less able to exist in the absence of air, that they do not carry fermentation so far, and that they stop or die before having transformed all their sugar. But these are merely differences in degree; the main point is to recognise that the relation between alcoholic fermentation and the exclusion of air is common to a long series of living organisms.

Yeast is one of the terms of this series, but not the last; for we have seen that after all it requires a little air, and I shall point out microbes, to which air is not only useless, but injurious.

Fermentation has ceased, I hope, to be for us an isolated and mysterious process, incapable of explanation or interpretation. It is the consequence of nutrition and of the existence of the cells under special conditions, which differ in most cases from those of their ordinary life, and to which yeast appears to easily adapt itself during the course of its fermenting career. But, as we have seen, yeast by its life in contact with air approaches nearly to the nature of ordinary plants; also that plants existing in carbonic acid possess the properties of yeast. Thus a continuous chain connects all these cells so dissimilar in appearance, their only difference being the fact that they present in greater or less degrees the two fundamental aspects of life with air, and life without air.

In the *Zeitschrift für das Gesammte Brauwesen* for 1888 there appeared a critical examination of the difference between Pasteur's and Hansen's views on the yeast question by Jorgensen – who is himself a high authority on this important subject – in which he gives great prominence to Hansen's views on fermentation. Ferdinand Hueppe, in a lengthy article replying to the above, claims to have put forth the same theory simultaneously with Hansen. Hueppe says:

The prominence thus given to Hanson's claims in a German journal startled me, as nowhere have Hansen's deserts been more unreservedly acknowledged than among ourselves. But why the opportunity should have been taken for a side-hit at

Koch and his pupils, I confess myself at a loss to understand. And I feel in duty bound to set the matter right, whilst making all due acknowledgment of the progress in the physiology and technology of fermentation for which we are indebted to Hansen. Amongst Koch's pupils I formerly stood alone in my devotion to problems of fermentative physiology. But my researches in milk decompositions were dependent on Koch only so far as regards the method; and on my later works Koch exerted no influence whatever. The charge of taking 'the same indefinite view' as Pasteur, therefore, points in a special manner to myself. Pasteur, in the study of lactic fermentation, which commenced in his famous 'Study of Fermentation,' endeavoured to show that every specific type of fermentation is the work of a special 'ferment'; and next that in this sense there is an alcoholic, a lactic, and a butyric fermentation. Subsequently he left this point somewhat obscure, and brought anaerobism more to the front. 'All fermentation is dependent on exclusion of air' was an oft-repeated watchword of the new French school of pathology. But, to improve on Pasteur, the nature of the ferment-organisms, in regard alike of their chemico-physiological conditions and their specific properties, must be kept in view. As regards the latter, the credit of having taken the first steps in advance unquestionably belongs to Brefeld. He was the first to follow, uninterruptedly from the germ, the morphology of organisms occurring in fermentations, and to show that fermentation and the resulting chemical changes were the work of *quasi*-specific micro-organisms, while as yet Pasteur had treated the subject very superficially. Among budding fungi the existence of surface and bottom yeasts led Pasteur to admit specific differences in yeasts, of which he recognised eight species. He thought also that more would be discovered, but he was rather vague on the subject – he supposed that all the cells in a yeast culture had certain properties in common, and also that every cell had its own distinctive characteristics ('des caractères propres qui la distinguent'), which by successive cultures might be made to originate new types. Thus in the same breath Pasteur talks of specific peculiarities and the variability of species of saccharomyces. All honour is due to Pasteur for having shown by his experiments in technical practice that industrial yeasts are rendered impure by bacteria, and that such bacterial organisms, some of which he described, may cause diseases in beers and wines. But this was not going far enough, and it was reserved for Hansen to show that wild yeasts are each derived from a single germ or spore. Hansen thus determined that wild and cultivated yeasts exhibit specific characteristics, and that different kinds of alcoholic fermentation depend on specifically distinct forms of saccharomyces. After several years of preliminary research Hansen published the first definite exposition of his labours in 1888 on bacteria. Cohn first addressed himself to supply the morphological omissions of Pasteur, and believed himself to have discovered – what, in part, was discovered quite independently by Lister – that bacterial decompositions are the work of eight different kinds of bacterial organisms. In this sense we learned to recognise an agent of lactic fermentation, another of butyric fermentation, and so forth. The unsatisfactory character of the method employed, and the view propounded in the meantime by Nageli, of the indefinite capacity differentiation of ferment organisms, led to my own investigations of the changes in milk. These were ready for the press at the end of March, 1883, and I never set eyes upon them again until the appearance of Part II of 'Mittheilungen aus Kaiserliche Gesundheit-amte', my prolonged absence from Germany debarring me from making any corrections therein. The work, however, was quite coeval with Hansen's. In it I showed by exact demonstration that definite types of decomposition are the work of definite *quasi*-specific micro-organisms, and that differences in such decompositions are due to specific biological differences in the organisms inducing them. In respect of budding fungi and bacteria, this more correct view was propounded by Hansen and myself at one and the same time, and quite independently of one another. And this fact alone is, I think, sufficient to show the impossibility of any serious incompatibility in our opinions.

The above extracts show that dissimilar views are still held by scientists of the new school of fermentative physiology, and the reader will see what reliance can as yet be placed upon the opinions of scientists engaged in this mysterious but all-absorbing theme of speculative theory – fermentation.

Sponging

Sponging is a blending together of flour, yeast and water, with the addition of salt, mixed into one substance, and practically carried through the successive stages at the proper degree of heat. No amount of theory will compass this, unless the operator has the practical part of his business well in hand.

SUNDAY SPONGING

Sunday night sponging is one of the baker's grievances, and is gradually drawing itself to the front and forcing itself both upon the trade and the public. That it is a hardship for bakers no one can gainsay.

Some twenty years ago a body of philanthropic gentlemen took up this matter, but their ideas were vague and proved to be illusory, as the system they advocated was based upon the old style of long and all-night-and-day sponging. The sudden atmospheric changes our country is subject to (and practical bakers who have charge of the sponging department know what care is required to guard against such changes) was one of the leading forces which helped to quash this much-needed reform. The mode adopted was as follows:–

To work up one sack of flour, the quantity of water required for a sponge, Scotch style, was heated to a certain degree, which would be, of course, pretty cool, but not sufficiently cold to starve the sponge. One quart of Parisian barm was added, with three pounds of salt; and the sponge was made pretty stiff. On the Sunday the foreman came and looked at the sponge, and if he thought it was working too quickly, or too slowly, he would regulate it accordingly, either taking sacks off, or putting sacks upon the trough; and there was always plenty of hot water that could be put under the trough if required. But if there was no change in the weather these things were seldom required.

This I know is too old-fashioned a plan for a modern bakery, and would not now be accepted by the trade.

My suggestion would be to abolish Sunday work altogether, adopt compressed yeast for Monday's work, and let one or two men (according to the size of the firm) come to the bakehouse about two hours before the usual time, and set a flying or quick sponge. It can be got ready in an hour and a half, and I am sure that bread worked in this way would, under a practical foreman, give satisfaction. Some, I know, are averse to German yeast, but there are plenty of so-called German yeasts of good quality made in England, that will answer quite as well. In my opinion it gives a nicer flavour; but those who are averse to working it (and I know of a good many in Scotland) should use Parisian barm. One or two men could be told off to do duty on Sunday, and they could get as many quarters as were required with Parisian barm, to be ready at an earlier hour on Monday morning. Then one or two should come early on Monday and set what sponges were required for the first round of bread. This arrangement would allow at least a few men to have Sundays for themselves; every little helps, and if any of these practices or modes, or any other arrangement of a feasible nature were once started, I am sure we have men in the trade skilful enough to bring this kind of sponging to a successful issue.

The recent movement in the baking trade, notably in England, Ireland, Scotland, and America, for lessening the number of hours a baker has to work, and for the alleviation of other grievances connected with the trade, is a sure sign that the baker is at last taking the initiative; success in the attempt to gain a higher position, and take a stand as a body of practical workmen, is merely a matter of time. Let us hope, then, that the day is not far distant when bakers will enjoy the rest of the Sabbath day, like any other tradesmen or civilised Christians. And let us work, as well as hope, for that end.

ON INCREASING AND DECREASING SPONGES

It frequently happens that after the afternoon sponges have been set, a material change takes place in the bread orders for the following day. Either an extra order has been booked, or the vans have not been so successful in their day's sales as the van-men anticipated; or the shop trade may fluctuate; or other things may happen that produce an accumulation of surplus bread. Take the first case, where an increase of the sponge already set is required. Suppose the extra bread required is twenty 4-lb loaves. Now each pail of water when worked with the requisite amount of flour produces, on an average, twenty 4-lb loaves. The salt required to season one pail of water (at the recognised rate of 3 lbs to the sack) would be a little under 10 ounces. When doughing add this extra pail of water and salt to the usual quantity of water required to take the sponge – all the water to be at an advanced temperature of eight degrees over the usual heat required. Then after the dough is made let it lie an extra half-hour before weighing off. This will give your required increase of twenty loaves. But the operator must not expect the bread made after this manner to have the same bold appearance as if the barm for this particular batch had not had the extra amount of salt and water to carry. The appearance of the dough, technically speaking, will have a greasy look, and it will be inclined to slide. On the other hand, suppose less bread is required and the sponge has to be taken down: allow the same proportion as for the increase, viz., twenty 4-lb loaves. Now, suppose it requires three pails of water at night and two pails in the morning with 3 lbs of salt to take up 20 stone of flour, one pail of water, with the corresponding amount of salt, must be kept from the sponge; the temperature to be eight degrees colder than the operator would take the sponge if the full complement of water was given; this will give the required result of twenty loaves less, and so on in proportion. I do not advocate this particular system, except in cases of emergency such as I have suggested at the beginning of this paragraph, and it particularly applies to the usual style of working in Scotland, where Parisian barm is the motive power used in fermenting sponges. In warm weather, when less salt and water is used than the amount of barm given is expected to ferment, great care and judgment is required or sour bread is likely to result. In England, where compressed yeast is the order of the day, the case is different, as any increase of orders can easily be met, and in a short time, by applying extra yeast to a quick or flying sponge. But any deviation from the required style or system recognised by the trade (providing that system is sound and practically based, and in harmony with the law of cause and effect) must have its bad effect on the flavour and general appearance of the bread.

SOURNESS IN BREAD

Of all the evils the baking trade has to contend with, sourness in bread is, I think, the worst. Some of my readers will very likely have heard the story of the two master bakers in Scotland.

One day Tammas Smith was walking down the high street of a Scottish town, when he saw a brother in trade, Geordie Robinson, pacing up and down in front of his own shop, evidently in anything but an agreeable frame of mind. When Tammas got up to Geordie, he said:–

'Weel, Geordie, hoo's a' wi' 'ye this mornin'? What makes ye luik sae agitated, mun?'

'Agitated!' exclaimed Geordie. 'Oor batch's oot, an' the breed's soor, an' I canna stand the smell o't i' my ain shop!'

No wonder that Geordie was agitated, for of all the smells that annoy a baker a 'soor' smell is the most aggravating. Certainly it is not Otto of Roses, Eau de Cologne, or Jockey Club. If anyone wishes to beg a favour from a baker, let him be sure to learn that his bread is sweet.

The causes of sourness in bread are so numerous that it is difficult to fix upon one specially. But its origin can be traced to germs of specific ferments, such as butyric and lactic ferments, which produce a certain amount of acidity; but the two causes which I consider most common are carelessness and want of cleanliness. If a bakehouse is not kept clean, and is not regularly whitewashed, the atmosphere becomes contaminated with germs, which enter into sponges, dough, barms, etc.; in fact, there is no telling where they may alight and propagate. They are as contagious as a fever, and it is as difficult a thing to expel them from a bakehouse as it is easy for them to enter one.

I remember, some years ago, in a small town named Maxwelltown, adjoining Dumfries, there was a rather large firm turning over between 60 and 70 sacks a week; and I well recollect what consternation arose when it was hinted that this firm's bread was sour, and had been so for a week. I did not believe the report at first, as the firm was noted for good, sweet, well-flavoured bread, and there were two good skilful men at the head of the bakery, though they were, for all I know, ignorant of chemistry. On inquiry the report proved to be too true; and they tried everything they knew to stop the ravages of these germs of specific ferments, such as fresh barm, fresh stores of barm, scalding out troughs and the barm tubs, hot lime, etc. – in fact, everything but the right thing. The sourness continued day after day for six weeks, till at last I believe they fumigated the bakehouse, whitewashed the walls, and used excessive cleanliness; then, and not till then, they exterminated these enemies of the baker.

Another cause of sourness in bread is too much warmth in setting the sponge, and allowing it to lie too long before it is taken. Still another lies in adding too warm water when taking up your sponge. Experience and a thermometer will obviate both these difficulties. Again, I have seen a sponge taken up in a healthy, ripe condition, and, some old scrap from a previous batch having been allowed to be mixed with it, it has turned out in anything but a satisfactory state. Another cause is impure or weak yeast or barm, most particularly so in flour and Parisian barm. But a good preventive of weakness in Parisian barm is to make it every day, if the amount required will allow you to do so.

Weak or bad flour is still another cause for sourness in bread. I have used flour so weak that I have not dared to let the sponge even turn, while with other flour it has had to be twice dropped before being taken. It may fitly be mentioned here that there is no hard and fast rule for a baker to go by, to know exactly when a sponge is ready, for all depends on the quality of the flour and the yeast employed. I find that sour milk is a great enemy to healthy dough, and when it is allowed to get mixed in barm or sponges, the impure germs are speedily propagated, and sour bread results. Causes for this disease in bread can be enumerated, but quite sufficient has been said to put the baker on his guard. Two things to be avoided let me again impress upon the baker – carelessness and uncleanliness.

The appearance of sour bread is the reverse of inviting. In some cases where it is sour it clings or dries on the sides of the loaves before it can be baked, and has a dull, glazed appearance.

Sometimes bread springs out of shape, and is liable to take no colour on the top, presenting an altogether boiled appearance, and turning out in a very untradesmanlike manner, with decided lack of finish.

Bread should always be thoroughly baked, though not baked too much. Underbaked bread has a tendency to sourness when it is kept, for the underbaked part in the centre of the loaf will be 'claggy' and is liable to ferment, and be quite unpalatable.

UNRIPE SPONGES

will next be treated upon – jimp, or still-born sponges, as I have sometimes heard them called.

Unripe sponges are the exact opposites of overworked sponges. A modern baker, however, seldom allows himself to be annoyed by their manufacture, as the spirit of competition is too keen to admit of the return to the old times of waiting and cooking unripe sponges. Still, cases occur when he cannot help himself, and he has a 'jimp' sponge.

Waiting for a sponge is like waiting for a train, and if one has any important business to transact the delay is both tedious and annoying. But if a baker attempts to take a sponge before it is ready he may be sure of the invariable result. If the sponge is very unripe, there is, as likely as not, the necessary heating of boards, a second rolling up, happed up with sacks, the waiting, and the gripping of the dough to see if it is getting any life into it or beginning to move; and after all the coaxing, heating and happing, the bread turns out heavy and sodden, with a dark pile and foxy appearance – in very truth, still-born. Thus a baker taking an unripe sponge is in no sense further forward than if he were content to leave it to work by itself into a healthy and properly ripe sponge. If the oven is in the usual degree of heat, the loaf's top crust is of a dirty black colour, and the bread when cut tastes claggy, as the protoplasm, or essence of life, has not been to any extent propagated in the ferments throughout the dough. Then again, an unripe sponge never gives that nice, healthy, inviting appearance one likes to note in bread, nor the nutty flavour one expects to taste in a well manipulated loaf.

Therefore, from unripe sponges and sour bread, good Lord, deliver us!

As a safeguard against both, I would advise brother tradesmen to stick to the one brand of yeast – if compressed – and flour, if both answer their purpose; for a skilful baker will soon know how to work both flour and yeast, and to extract from them, as regards strength, colour and flavour, all that is in them. Do not, if it can be avoided, shift from one brand to another, as it is in the constant change of flour and yeast that sourness has the chance of entering. Some yeasts work with a fierce, rank strength; others, again, work in a feeble, dead-slow manner. The same remarks are nearly applicable to flour. Do not, unless compelled, keep continually changing, or your chances of success are very remote.

FLOUR FERMENTS

As we have discarded potatoes in ferments, we will proceed to give the formula for flour ferments, which are a great help to bakers, should they have the misfortune to be working soft flour. It likewise imparts a nice flavour to the bread.

To make twenty stone of flour into bread: See that your ferment tub is nice and clean. Put into it a small scoop of flour – about four pounds. Put two gallons of boiling water upon the flour in the tub; add, when the flour is thoroughly scalded, sufficient cold water to cool it down to 90°F; take a gallon of store or Parisian barm, and mix all together; then keep it covered with a sack in a warm place till ready. This is generally set between ten and eleven in the morning, and taken at four in the afternoon.

German yeast can be used in the flour ferment instead of Parisian barm. Ferment eight ounces to the same quantity of water and flour.

QUARTER SPONGES TO TAKE UP ONE SACK OF FLOUR

Put one gallon of water at about 90°F into the quarter tub with half a gallon of Parisian barm, and mix all together into a good stiff sponge. Keep in a warm place, covered with a sack, till ready. Set at one o'clock; to be taken at four. Then add sufficient water, at the required temperature, with 2 lbs of salt; thoroughly mix all together, and make a good dry sponge. When the sponge is ready, add the requisite quantity of water and salt, which should be about 6 gallons of water and from 1 lb to 1½ lb of salt.

Before proceeding to give the modern method of sponging, let me impress upon my readers the necessity for using rice flour, mixed with fine flour, for dusting and rolling up. Never use it for moulding, as it gives a dull, dark appearance to the crust of the loaf when baked; but for dusting the troughs and boards, and in rolling up – especially if the sponge be unripe, or when soft flour is employed – rice flour is invaluable. Also let me state that seventeen gallons of water are required to take up twenty stone of flour. This is the average, the amount varying with the strength of the flour. Let the baker see that the compressed yeast is not roughly handled; it is sometimes spoiled if dropped upon the ground. Too much care in handling cannot be taken. Keep it, also, in a cool place of even temperature, especially in warm weather.

When milk is required for bread, such as milk bread, diet bread, etc., buttermilk should be used; but if it cannot be procured condensed milk can be substituted, although it does not answer so well, as it does not contain sufficient acid to counteract the soda.

When condensed milk is used the bread must be baked in a sharper oven than if it had been doughed with buttermilk. The baker will be amply repaid for the greatest care and attention in these matters, for has he not the satisfaction of knowing that he has done his best (and angels can do no more), and that the bread produced must be of a superior quality to what it would have proved had he left its manufacture to chance or accident?

Let it also be remembered that more salt is required to season strong flour than for ordinary or weak flour, to produce a loaf of equal texture, on account of the extra quantity of water needed to work up such flour.

Modern Method of Sponging

In firms of any note the old style of sponging would not be tolerated. When it was necessary to prepare the search for the potato ferment, and cautiously pour the liquid, or ferment, into the search before squeezing the unbroken potatoes (if by chance any should be underboiled), the operator was afraid lest any potato skins should get into the sponge water, and was compelled, if by accident this happened, to hunt in the water for the offending skin with vigour and persistency, while the sponge water was cooling and time being wasted.

The modern baker goes to work in a more methodical way. To convert a sack of flour into bread the whole must be emptied into the trough, and partitioned off with a sprint board to suit the sponge required. Take twelve gallons of water heated to the required temperature (90°) and dissolve from ten to sixteen ounces of yeast, according to its strength, and mix it amongst the liquid for the sponge; dissolve 2 lbs of salt in the liquid and set a good, beaten, dry sponge. In the morning – or at such time as it is taken up – add six gallons of water with 1½ lbs of salt broken well in the sponge; then make into dough.

The reader will notice that ½ lb of salt more than the recognised quantity has been recommended, because, for myself, I prefer well-worked sponges, to obtain what flavour I can, and to keep, by the extra amount of salt, a pile on the bread.

All the following methods of sponging are adapted for either hand or machine doughing.

QUICK OR FLYING SPONGES

These can be got ready sponged in from one to one and a half hours' time, according to the quality of the yeast and the temperature of the bakehouse. These points should always be kept in mind. After one sack of flour has been put into the trough, make a sprint; add twelve gallons of water at about 100°F; then dissolve in half a gallon of the sponge liquid 2 lbs of yeast (compressed yeast is here referred to), and set a weak sponge, about the consistency of sponge-cake batter; let this rise till you think it is ready; and then add 6 gallons of water at the same temperature as the sponge, with 3½ lbs of salt dissolved in it; break well in and dough. This sponge, when thoroughly ready, requires quick, sharp manipulation in its removal to the oven. This method of working makes a really capital loaf.

OVERNIGHT SPONGING IN LARGE FIRMS

For every one and a half pails, i.e. about four and a half gallons of water, allow 5½ oz of yeast and 5½ oz of salt. Any required quantity may be set after this method, but it must be remembered that the larger the sponge the less yeast proportionately is needed – for instance, if for three pails 10 oz is used, for four and a half pails 14 oz is required, and so on. On taking up this sponge in the morning, for every pail and a half, or four and a half gallons, of water set in the sponge, one pail of water and 1 lb of salt must be allowed. Good bread by this, as by the last method, is made.

TO MAKE A FULL SPONGE WITH PARISIAN BARM, WITHOUT QUARTER OR FERMENT

For a 40-stone batch, put 20 gallons of water at the required heat into the trough, and add 3 gallons of Parisian barm with 4 lbs of salt dissolved in the liquid. Make into a sponge – (see 'Modern Method of Sponging') – and when ripe put to it 12 gallons of water at the requisite temperature, with 2¼ lbs of salt dissolved in part of the liquid; break well in, and make into dough.

HOW TO SET A SPONGE

In large breadmaking firms where the doughing machine is not used, two men, and sometimes three, are required to set a sponge. The following is the proper method: when the requisite quantity of flour is in the trough, or, in the trade vernacular, 'when the trough is pitched', the heat of the water ascertained by the thermometer to be correct, and the salt and yeast added, the first man begins operations by drawing a quantity of the flour into the liquor, and his assistant starts mixing it. Then both men mix the loose flour and the liquor together, and the flour that remains to be taken in is added. Care is here necessary to see that no dry flour adheres to the bottom of the trough. When all the flour and liquor is thoroughly mixed, throw the sponge from one end of the trough to the other, so as to take up any slack sponge that may remain in it; repeat this until you have both ends of the trough clear. Dust the top of the sponge with flour, and then throw the sides of the sponge into the middle, finishing this process by giving it a thorough good beating. This is done by placing both arms half-way through the sponge, keeping the hands nearly touching one another, lifting as much sponge in the arms as can conveniently be held, and throwing it to the back or side of the trough; continue throwing from end to end of the trough till the sponge is nice and dry. You may now rub the sponge from your arms, and scrape down the sides and ends of the trough. Draw the scrapings into the centre, and finish by bringing the back part of the sponge to the front; give the top a dust of flour, and rub the flat of the hands down between the sponge and the sides and ends of the trough. It should be noted that weak flours require tighter sponges than ordinary or strong flours.

This is the first important stage in the interesting process of making bread with compressed yeast.

HOW TO A TREAT OVER-WROUGHT SPONGES

The following is the system adopted by many bakers: Allow an extra half-pound of salt to every twenty stone of flour on taking up the sponge. Use all speed and every reasonable expedient to get the batch into the oven, and see that the oven is from six to ten degrees over the usual heat. This method of working strong sponges is to check fermentation.

A method put forth by a new school of bakers – and one which to a practical baker seems altogether inconsistent with the rule of cause and effect – is to add more yeast to an already overworked sponge. I have repeatedly tested this method with small quantities of sponge, but obtained very unsatisfactory results. Our views on fermentation and breadmaking are steadily changing; but to place a healthy body with an unhealthy one and expect favourable results is, so far as we at present know, unreasonable and altogether opposed to scientific research.

A specific or antidote for over-worked sponges which I can recommend, and one which I have tested with good results, is as follows: – To every twenty stone of flour dissolve six ounces of carbonate of soda with the water and salt required to take the sponge up. This will improve both the taste and the bloom of the bread; but it will not – nor will any other method – make sour bread sweet.

The Manipulation of Dough

HOW TO MAKE DOUGH BY HAND

Let the operator who has charge of the dough-making department see that sufficient flour is put into the trough to take up all the sponge. This can easily be done by observing the quantity of sponge that is set, and the strength of the flour used. Avoid the happy-go-lucky method that is followed in some establishments in making dough by hand – that is, adding scoopful after scoopful of flour to get the dough the required size after it is half made, as the result of this practice is to waste time, to tire out the operators, and to produce dough finished in an untradesmanlike manner. After mixing the flour in the sponge, shake the whole mass thoroughly together, for on this shaking process depend the quality and the easy manipulation of the dough. When the lot is well shaken, and no scrappy parts remain, cut the dough from end to end of the trough – (see 'Method of Cutting Dough') – and let each cut part be well spread before placing one on top of the other. By cutting and spreading it three times from one end of the trough to the other, the dough should be well made. By this process, and with efficient workmen, a batch of sixty stone of flour can easily be made into dough in fifteen minutes. When the dough is having the last turn before finishing, use a mixture of rice-flour and flour, in equal quantities, to dust the bottom of the trough with, so that the dough will lift freely when throwing it on to the table. Before starting to make the dough, the operator should rub his arms over with melted lard. This will give him more freedom of action, as the dough that adheres to his arms will then the more easily rub off.

To be a good dough-maker, one must know exactly what to do, and when and how to do it.

METHOD OF CUTTING DOUGH

When it is found requisite to remove the dough from the trough, or when the dough is made by the hand in the trough, the operator will find it of great advantage to cut the dough in a slanting direction instead of in the old recognised manner, viz., in a straight line. If the old, unsystematic style of cutting is adopted, the mass that the part is cut from soon overlaps and mixes again with the cut part, necessitating greater labour to remove the part that is cut than if it had been done obliquely. Although this is apparently a simple little wrinkle, it will really prove of great benefit to the baker when making or cutting dough from the trough; and where this method is not already adopted I would strongly urge my brother craftsmen to at least give it a trial, as it will save a great deal of labour, especially in large firms.

HOW TO WEIGH OFF A BATCH OF BREAD

In large bakeries a weigher-off requires an assistant as cutter-out, and it is of the utmost importance that both men should be quick in perception and thoroughly practical, for on this department of the manufacture of bread depend, in a great measure, the profits that accrue to the employer.

The weigher-off takes the shell-plate of the scales between his thumb and fingers, the bottom of the plate resting on his fingers, with his thumb on the top, so that when the dough is placed upon it he will, if he has the lightness of touch requisite in a good weigher-off, know at once, by the pressure of the scale-plate on his thumb and fingers, if the dough requires adding to or taking from it. He should also be able to tell by the weight of the cut dough as he lifts it from the table to the scale-plate. The most important thing is to know exactly how much is required to make the dough the proper weight, and to make one motion of the hand finish the operation. That is, if the loaf is two ounces short of the weight required, the weigher must guess the quantity at once, and not put four ounces on when only two are required, as this entails a waste of time and is most untradesmanlike. The same applies when the dough is overweight. With two practical men at the scales, if the cutter-out is an expert at this part of his trade, weighing off dough becomes merely a matter of form, as the weight of the cut pieces has very seldom to be altered. Two such men can very easily keep two, and sometimes three others rolling up loaves of dough at their very quickest. A modern bakery of any size ought to have two or three good scalesmen, so as to accelerate the work and make the financial part of the business both accurate and reliable.

HOW TO ROLL UP LOAVES OF DOUGH

This is the first process the dough undergoes when the batch is being weighed off. Take in each hand one of the pieces weighed, keeping the cut or moist part of the dough lying on the table, and the scrappy or dry part, if any, towards the top. Then with the heel of each hand press the sides of the dough on the table, and with the fingers turn the sides into the centre; repeat this till each piece is round and the dough has a nice clear skin, and then draw the close of the dough into the centre underneath – the close will then be imperceptible. The rolled-up loaves are now placed on dusted boards holding from thirty to forty 2 lb loaves; the boards are then placed one on top of another, or run on shelves in a press made for the purpose, and left until the moulding process is begun.

Four ounces of flour and rice-flour, mixed in equal proportions, should be placed about sixteen inches from the front of the table, to keep the loaves dry while the baker is rolling them up. Two ounces of flour should also be placed at the same distance on the table in front of the baker to keep the loaves dry while moulding.

HOW TO MOULD A SQUARE LOAF

After the dough has been brought through its various stages of fermentation, moulding a loaf is the next most difficult process in our trade. Take the dough firmly in your hands, making sure that the moist or 'green' part, which is to be found on one side of the rolled-up loaves of dough, is next the table. This little wrinkle is requisite to secure a good skin. The closed part of the dough should be clear of the table, and is generally at the upper far part of the loaf. Commence by throwing the two sides into the centre of the loaf. Then draw the back part squarely into the centre, joining it with the heel of the hand, giving it a firm bash, and then rolling it with both hands into the half mould. The close of the loaf is now uppermost, with each side a little narrower than the centre. Then bash or press out the half-moulded loaf and throw the side parts over each other in the centre; again bash and close in. Closing in is done with 2-lb loaves by bringing the back part of the dough to the front part and firmly rolling the dough back. Then once more bring the two parts together, bashing or squeezing them, and at the same time squaring off the loaf. In moulding square loaves the body should have an easy movement. The manipulator must have the utmost command of his arms, at the same time keeping the loaf firmly in his hands during the whole process. By this method a nice square loaf can be made, having both the requisites of a well-moulded loaf, viz., firmness and a nice silky skin. Some experts mould a loaf in each hand. This does very well for square tin loaves, but I do not approve of it for moulding square loaves for oven-bottom batches. Let a man be ever so clever or expert in moulding a square loaf with each hand, there is always a lack of firmness, texture, and artistic finish with this method of moulding. To mould a good loaf requires conception and practice.

HOW TO MOULD A ROUND LOAF

Begin as for a square loaf, that is, by having your moist, or, in trade language, 'green' part of the dough next to the table. Divide the dough into two parts, having the right hand piece smaller than the left. Now chaff this into two round pieces – (see 'How to Roll up Loaves of Dough,' chaffing being the same process, only more expeditious) – with a close in each part no larger than a pigeon's eye. Place the two closes together; then bash the loaf with the heel of the right hand, and press the elbow of the right arm into the centre of the loaf, and your moulding process is finished. This, like the preceding style for moulding square loaves, requires practice and strength to mould the loaves firm, and to give them a silky and suitable texture. Learners should try to properly half mould first, leaving the finish of the loaf to those more able to accomplish the art.

MOULDING AND BOARDING

Until very recently no machine had been invented to take the place of hand moulding, and as it is not in general use it is very requisite for the foreman to see that the man he engages or recommends is a good moulder, as it is on the manner in which his work is done that a great deal of the success expected from the ovenman depends.

If the dough is of the ordinary consistency, the moulder should be able to finish his loaf in a quick, tradesmanlike manner; and the loaf, if square oven-bottom batch, should be square and firm; the skin, likewise, of the loaf should be smooth and silky, not cracked and soft, with long stringy marks here and there on the surface, or, as it often is, bazen-looking and rough. There is as much skill required in moulding a loaf well as in any hand labour in baking I know of.

If there are one or two moulding who throw up their finished loaves to the boarder in a soft state, this proof of their want of skill is soon discovered by either the setter-up or ovenman, who as a rule are not slow in letting the moulder's inefficiency be known in the proper quarter. And the ovenman is only doing his duty in thus protecting himself and his employer. Where two or three loaves are run at a time, it is annoying, to say the least of it, for him to see two good, firm loaves and one unfinished one on the same peel, the bad one most likely running on to the oven bottom before he can get them into the course. Nor is he able to make his batch as square as it should be, as loaves moulded in this way throw him, as they say, 'off his course'. The same thing applies in the case of round or cottage bread – with this difference, that cottage dough should be tighter, and the deficiency is not so apparent. It does not matter so much for pan bread so long as it has a finished appearance and good skin, as the dough, after being put into the tins, is not handled till baked. Still, for long pans, to bring out a good, showy loaf with a nice pile, the loaf must be well moulded.

I have boarded for men who were moulding a cottage batch, and have actually seen the loaf with the close on the top, side, or anywhere but where it ought to be. Such experiences are, of course, exceptions; but the proper methods cannot be driven into men who have not the perception to see their utility.

A man must be very expert before he can become a good boarder. In a modern bakery there are so many men allowed for each boarder that all his knowledge and energy are needed to keep the table clear. As the finished loaves come up he has to arrange them in rows of eight or nine, sides uppermost. Every third loaf is greased before being put on to the board, and they are arranged in rows to fit it; as each row is completed, the front ends of all the loaves in that row are greased, and so on till the board is filled. Next the tops of the loaves are docked, and they are put away in their places till the batch is moulded. At a given time the ovenman sees that the ovens are shuffled out, and up-sets are in their places round the oven. He begins to run the batch, usually eighteen or twenty 4 lbs in a course, or twenty-four to twenty-six 2 lbs. And it is very interesting for an outsider, or one not belonging to the baking trade, to see how skilfully and speedily some bakers can arrange the loaves.

Round or cottage bread is easier to board and run than square batches. A considerable amount of practice is necessary before proficiency can be obtained in this part of the baking trade.

SETTING OR RUNNING BATCHES

A good ovenman has always a certain amount of deference shown him in a modern bakery, and this is not to be wondered at when we think how much the quality and ultimate appearance of the bread depend on his knowledge and skill. It is painful to see a man working at an oven whose proper occupation would be grooming horses or working in a brick-field. Employers who are not practical men cannot imagine how much against their own interests it is to engage such. A batch of bread put into an evenly heated oven depends in a great measure for its flavour and weight on the dexterity of the baker. If, for instance, ten to fifteen minutes are required to set an ovenful of loaves – or, as we should say in trade parlance, a batch of bread – and the same time to draw them, then the first course of loaves put into the oven is consequently from twenty to thirty minutes longer baking than the last peelful put in. Thus the first two or three courses are more or less overbaked, and the weight of the first will be less than the last, as there is less moisture, and naturally less substance. Besides this, the loaf cuts in a crumbly fashion, and is dry to eat and deficient of that nice, mellow, glutenous taste and nutty flavour characteristic of a good loaf. It will thus be seen that it behoves employers to secure good, active, skilful ovenmen to turn out bread that will please the eye and gratify the palate.

To secure an equal baking in running a batch of pan bread into the oven, no great skill or extraordinary art is required; only speed. I have repeatedly run 180 4-lb tin loaves into the oven in two minutes and a half, and filled three ovens with 180 4-lb loaves each in eight minutes, two handing forward and one peeling on. This of course was not our usual time, and was only done, so to speak, out of bravado, to ascertain in what time it really could be done. But though it is an easy matter for an ordinary baker of some celerity to run a batch of tin bread, the running of an oven-bottom batch of square, round, or cottage loaves is quite another thing. To ensure success with these a man must be an expert in the handling of the peel, and must have a quick eye, a steady hand, and quick perceptions all round. For a man of this stamp it is essential to have an assistant who is a good setter-up, i.e. one who squares up the loaves and prepares them for the ovenman, or puts them on the peel ready for the oven. In Glasgow, where they are in great request, such men are paid really good wages.

Plain and Fancy Bread, etc.

The common bread of Great Britain, or bread for general use, may be divided into three classes: (1) Wheaten bread, made of the very finest flour and generally called 'firsts'; (2) Household bread, made of somewhat coarser flour and usually called 'seconds' and (3) Brown bread, made in various qualities.

The finest flour is entirely separated from the bran or husks; the second is not thoroughly so; while from the coarsest flour the broad bran only is removed.

Coarse bread, made from what the Scotch called overhead flour, was formerly much used in Scotland. This quality of bread had a nice, nutty flavour. It can be made by the same method as given for the manufacture of full sponges.

Brown bread is admitted to be our lowest class of bread. The baker has also so many chances of adulterating it, though I do not say this is always done.

Competition in the making of bread is now so keen that a practical baker is sometimes at his wit's end to produce a loaf that will be at once agreeable to the taste and pleasing to the eye. But he is still not so sorely handicapped in the race and struggle for trade and custom as the outsiders who follow the commercial pursuit of supplying bread to the masses. I here allude to bread companies, stores, grocers, and other dealers who make and sell bread – the two latter sometimes selling at a loss, in order to advertise their other commodities.

The first-named – the bread companies – we can partly tolerate, as in many cases a certain amount of the profit is shared with the employees; and, to judge by the signs of the times, we may expect that the bulk of the baking trade will eventually fall into their hands. This would be a boon to journeymen; but till such a time comes let the trade protect industrial effort in a reasonable manner, so as not to clog the interests of employers or employed.

Grocers and other dealers have not the same chance of success in dressing their shop windows with nice, clean, showy bread as a modern practical baker has. I have seen bread jumbled anyhow and anywhere, amongst paraffin oil, matches, soap, candles, and even blacking. How tempting to a customer such a display must be! This shows that a real baker has a great advantage over a make-believe one, who, instead of sticking to the occupation fate has chosen for him, goes poaching about, and, figuratively speaking, poking his finger into everybody's pie and filching a piece out of every dish he sets his eyes upon, unmindful of the harm such selfish action causes to practical tradesmen. Happily, such individuals often get their fingers burnt, but that does not deter others from following the same selfish course.

I now propose to describe a class of bread which is second to none in the market. The following are my methods of preparation, as adapted to the requirements of the establishment in which I am engaged. Anyone properly attending to the instructions here given will be well pleased with the results; there are no better or more expeditious methods known to the trade.

VIENNA BREAD

This I claim to be our highest grade of white bread, and one not affording opportunities for adulteration.

Take 8 lbs of flour (Hungarian best brand), three quarts of milk and water in equal proportions, 3½ oz of compressed yeast, and 1½ oz of salt. Mix the water (warm) with the milk so that the final temperature may be about 85°F; dissolve the yeast in this, and with a little of the flour make a flour ferment, which should stand for about one hour; then add the remainder of the flour and the salt, and thoroughly knead all together. Let this lie for two hours and a half, and work off, prove, and bake. If a jet of steam can be introduced into the oven the bread will get nicely glazed.

FANCY COTTAGE LOAVES

This class of bread, and the fancy kinds following, must be sponged with Hungarian flour, and doughed with it also. 'PWM' is a suitable brand. Machine the dough to a good stiffness in the mixer; let it lie to prove for an hour and a half, and then throw it upon the table and weigh off at 1½ lb, if for cottages, to sell at threepence each. Roll the loaves up into boards, using a little rice flour for dusting and rolling up; after all are worked up cover with either boards or sacks; prove one hour and start to mould. Split each piece of dough into two parts, one considerably larger than the other; mould separately with a fine, silky skin, and place the smaller part upon the larger; punch with the palm of your hand, and dig your elbow into the centre of the loaf; place on boards a little distance apart, egg over the top, and prove in proving press. Do not prove them too much, or they will fall in the oven. When ready wash again with egg, and run two at a time on the oven bottom, just allowing them to touch and no more. The oven is in the best condition for baking these just after a tin batch has been turned out. This method, if properly adhered to, should afford satisfaction.

HOW TO MAKE TWISTS

Weigh off at 1 lb 6 oz for threepence. Go through the same process as for cottages. When the dough is ready to work off divide each piece into three equal parts, and roll each part out to a length of four or five inches. When this has been done, again roll out each part about fourteen inches long, tapering at the ends and thickening in the middle; now attach the three pieces to each other, end to end; then plait, as it were, the side pieces round the centre one till the twist is complete, tapering at the ends as before; place on sheet tins and egg over the top; prove as before, and again egg. Bake them in the same kind of oven as for cottages.

COBURGS, OR COBS

make a fine, showy line when nicely got up, and look well in a shop window. Weigh off the required quantity from cottage dough and prove for the same time on boards. After they are rolled up as for cottages, take one in each hand and mould round to a fine, silky skin; place on boards a little apart; wash over with water and prove. The time for proving must be left to the operator's practical judgment, for much depends on the heat of the prover, the ripeness of the sponge, and the temperature of the bakehouse. When ready, wash over with water again; then with a sharp knife cut across the middle to the depth of one inch, and again at right angles to form a cross; run them on to the oven bottom, a little apart; keep the door closed for twenty minutes, and bake them to a deep, golden brown. Weigh at 1 lb 10 oz for threepence. When these loaves are got up to perfection they are crusty all round, and have the appearance of a full-blown rose.

COMMON VIENNA LOAVES

Prepare dough as for cottages. Mould the loaf nice and firm, making it square and about twelve inches long, and properly finish it. Cut the top of the loaf, just breaking the skin of the dough, from end to end; then cross-wise from opposite corners. Place on tins, egg them over, and prove. When ready, egg over again and bake in a nice heat. Weigh at 1 lb 8 oz for fourpence.

MELVIN LOAVES

The dough used for these should be a shade slacker than that used for the above, but not as slack as for tin dough. Proceed as for cottages; then mould the dough up round, not forgetting to have a fine skin on the loaf at the finish. Egg the loaf all over, and with a knife mark all round from bottom to top; then reverse the cutting to form a diamond shape. Place on sheet tins and cover with the Melvin tins; prove, and bake in a good oven. Weigh at 1 lb 10 oz for fourpence.

By practice alone can one tell when these loaves are proved enough, as they cannot be seen when once put to prove. My method is to knock the tins with the knuckles; in a short time you will get to know the difference of sound, as the loaf rises and gradually fills the tin in proving.

SANDWICH LOAVES

This is another nice line, and will greatly help a display in the window. Hungarian flour is used in doughing and sponging, but the dough must be very much slacker than for cottages, as that used for these loaves is technically known as tin dough. Clean your tins, and then slightly grease them. The common size is 3½ lbs for sixpence, or 7 lbs for a shilling. But, of course, the weight of all these loaves is regulated by the price of the flour. Less time for proving will be required than for cottages, as this dough, being of a softer nature, sooner matures. Fill your tins at above weights; prove, and bake in a rather brisk oven.

FRENCH LOAVES

are made from the same kind of dough as sandwich loaves, weighed at 4 lbs and 2 lbs each. When proved, a flat piece of sheet iron or a flat scraper is used to cut the dough across the middle of the longest part of the loaf; press the scraper or cutter down through the dough, touching the bottom of the tin. As soon after cutting as possible put the loaves into the oven so that the cut just made may not join up again; the loaf will then leave the oven with a nice incision in the centre. This class, when properly got up, looks well. One penny more per 4-lb loaf is charged than for the ordinary fine loaf. It is well worth it.

BOX ROLLS

Use the dough as for sandwich loaves, proceeding in the same way. Weigh off at 1¾ lb for threepence, or 3½ lbs for sixpence; prove, and bake in a sharp oven. The tins used must be square, and fitted in size to the above weights. An ordinary 2-lb or 4-lb tin will not do. The operator should bear in mind that Hungarian flour, prepared according to my instructions, will take a higher bloom and appear more 'topy', as our technical friends phrase it, if baked in an oven of the same temperature as is used for ordinary bread.

PULLED BREAD

Take a new-baked loaf, and, either with the fingers or a large fork, pull the inside into pieces about the size of an egg; place them on a clean sheet tin, and bake in a sound oven. When baked let the pieces be of a nice brown colour, and as dry and crumpy as rusks. Pulled bread is sold at one shilling per pound, and is mostly used in large hotels.

SODA BREAD

Eight pounds of flour (Hungarian), 3 oz of tartar, 2 oz of soda, 2 oz of salt. Sift through the sieve; make a bay in the flour, and dough with buttermilk. Make a nice working dough, and weigh off at 1¾ lb for threepence. Put on a flat sheet tin, egg on top, place round tins over, and bake.

AERATED BREAD

Properly speaking, this is a substitute for aerated bread, as the baker has not the mechanical appliances for forcing the gas into the dough, as in aerated bread. The following is the method: for every pound of Hungarian flour use a bottle or gill of aerated soda-water, and allow salt at the rate of two ounces to the stone, which will only be a small pinch to a pound. Empty the soda-water into a basin; as quickly as possible throw flour upon it; mix and get as much gas as you can, and in a few minutes put it into the oven. This is not so showy as the original aerated bread, and the reason is obvious. The soda-water should be as brisk as possible.

PATENT OR UNLEAVENED BREAD

Twenty pounds of Hungarian flour, 8 oz of cream of tartar, 5 oz of soda, 1 lb of lard, 1 lb of sugar, and 6 oz of salt. Dough with churned milk into a nice-sized dough. Weigh at 1¾ lb for threepence. Grease each loaf all round, and put four into a pan made for the purpose, with a fitting lid. The pan should be thirteen inches in diameter and seven inches deep. When these are baked they should be nice, showy, three-cornered loaves.

HOME-MADE BREAD

Put one stone of flour in a pan or basin; dissolve two ounces of good yeast in a gill and a half of warm water, and place them in a hole made in the centre of the flour. Stir about four ounces of flour amongst the yeast and water and let it rise in a warm place. When it is ready, which will be when it has a nice cauliflower-like head, dissolve two ounces of salt in a tea-cup of warm water, and pour it upon the ferment. Proceed to add as much flour as may be requisite to make all into a nice dough, and put it in a warm place to rise. When risen, divide it into the required sizes and bake the dough in tins, giving it a slight proof first. It would be as well for bakers to remember that half an ounce of salt is required for a four-pound loaf. Different classes of flour require more, but this is the average.

FAMILY, OR HOME-BAKED BREAD, MADE WITH BREWERS' BARM

An expeditious and simple method of making bread for a small family, or for wholesale bakers who supply home-made bread, is as follows:–

Put a bushel of flour, all but four pounds, into a tub or pan, and in winter warm it near the fire or oven. Take a pint of good, fresh brewers' barm, with a small quantity of warm water; pour the water and yeast gently into a hole in the middle of the flour, mix the water and yeast with sufficient flour to make it into a stiff batter, and cover it up in a warm place till it has risen. Then dissolve in warm water six ounces of salt, and add it to the batter with sufficient water to make all into a nice mellow dough. After it has again risen make it into loaves, giving it a slight proof, and bake in a good oven.

I may here observe that practice and sound judgment are needed to properly regulate the heat of the oven. Dough that is going too freely requires a sharper oven than ordinary dough. Pan or tin loaves requiring proving should have a good sharp oven, both to check the fermentation and impart flavour to the bread. Cold ovens are useless for bread baking, for bread thus baked looks boiled, and always has a bad flavour.

NAMES OF VARIOUS LOAVES MADE IN BRITAIN

Firstly, there is 4-lb batch, square and round; then 2-lb batch, square and round – although the round is called cottage in some districts. Further, there are pan or tin loaves; sandwich, square and round, from 1½ lb to 14 lbs; French, twist and Vienna loaves; Coburg loaves, cobs, and cottages; the heart loaves in Edinburgh called French; Melvins, crusty and crumby loaves, tin cakes, Hungarian loaves, and others. The most popular of these have, I think, been enumerated.

HOT ROLLS IN ENGLAND

Rolls are not in such great demand in England as in Scotland, owing, I suppose, to the fact that the English housewife is able to make so many different tit-bits and choice morsels for her own table. It is a notable fact that, with the exception of those working in our large centres of population, very few bakers in England make rolls – at any rate, very few in comparison with the quantity sold in Scotland. French rolls are mostly used here; they are weighed at various weights, and halved, chaffed, and stented out – i.e., made sharp or pointed at the ends; placed on French roll tins; proved, and baked in a sharp oven. They must be well baked, or they will not rasp as all French rolls should.

Next are plain rolls, moulded up square and placed in rows on edged tins; each course is greased at the ends, so that they may readily separate after they are baked. They are worked off in this manner, proved, and baked.

Cob rolls also are weighed at various weights, the dough being a little tighter than for plain or French rolls; they are chaffed up round, and one part placed on the top of the other, the uppermost being the smallest, and the thumb is pressed into them to hold them together. They are either placed on tins, proved, and baked on the tins; or placed on warm boards, proved, and run on the oven bottom.

In some watering places during the season when visitors are present, it is becoming common to order from the baker rolls of different varieties, such as horse-shoes, twists, turnovers, cobs, and Jews' loaves, entailing an extraordinary amount of labour on the baker, and causing him to waste precious time – which he can ill afford to do at that time of the year.

SCOTCH ROLLS

Ah! Scotland is the place where rolls *par excellence* can be obtained, from the diminutive loaf, top and bottom, to the large penny 'swine', a large roll which was first chaffed, then stented, placed on a warm board to prove, and dusted with flour before being run into the oven. It had another name – 'Penny Dag'. I have sold them under the name of 'Coarse Geordies', but this was in the south of Scotland, and people's tastes in names may have altered. The majority of bakers in Scotland do a fair trade in rolls. Scotchmen are like Americans – they like hot bread: whether it is from the coldness of the climate or a natural taste is a matter for conjecture; but the fact remains that they like rolls, especially hot ones. In ordinary shops the roll dough is taken from the sponge in the morning before the extra water is added; or enough is taken from the sponge water at night during the sponging, and set in a somewhat warmer place (either at the trough end, or in a boat or tub for the purpose), as the sponge must be well worked for rolls. In firms where a large quantity is made a separate sponge is set for them. There are baps, long rolls, round, plain, cottages, etc. They are made as follows: After the dough is headed up, as it is called, the rolls are weighed off. Each man then takes a weighed-off portion, halves it, takes the parts one in either hand, and chaffs them – either long or round. Let us take the long first. The boards on which they are proved should fit the oven. While a boy is heating the boards a man starts to stent them out; the boards are then dusted with a mixture of rice flour and flour, and the rolls are placed on them in rows, touching each other, but with the ends at least one inch apart. They are put aside to prove as each board is filled; when proved, which should take from half to three-quarters of an hour, each row is cut in two, or through the middle. The oven man then takes them carefully and quickly in his hand and places them on the peel, and then runs them on the oven bottom. But he must be careful in lifting not to knock the proof out of them.

PLAIN ROUND ROLLS

are chaffed round, placed touching one another on an edge pan, proved, and baked.

BAPS

is the name given to rolls peculiar to some districts. They are chaffed up like long rolls, but in stenting they are knocked out flat with the hand, placed on warm boards, then cut in the centre with a sharp knife, washed on the top and put apart to prove. They are baked on the oven bottom.

There are a good many Glasgow scones, as they are called, that come under the head of rolls, but as this book treats on bread exclusively they must be omitted.

Brown Bread, Wheat meal, Rye, etc.

The brown bread craze I take to be exploded; if I could have my own way I would see that those who advocate the feeding of the masses on brown bread were fed on it themselves, until they should exclaim 'Hold! enough!' We should hear less then of the benefits of brown bread. That it suits some constitutions better than white I do not for a moment doubt or deny; let those whom it suits stick to their brown bread, just as some affect vegetables and despise beef. But to enable men to stand the strain of physical labour or excessive brain work, I strongly recommend good, wholesome, well-made white bread. I am sure that the inhabitants of Great Britain would compare favourably as regards strength or endurance with the much-lauded ancients, who are supposed to have lived entirely on brown bread or crushed wheat. Take, for instance, Captain Nares's expedition to the North Pole. Can we refer to any better test of strength and endurance than was there displayed? They were not fed on brown bread, but on unleavened, hard, white bread. Going to the other extreme for another instance, look at our own soldiers in the Soudan – what extremes of heat and fatigue they were subjected to in the burning, thirsty desert! They were not fed on brown bread; and I say again that the notion of the support derived from brown bread is an exploded theory, and its upholders cannot prove their position either scientifically or argumentatively. If these people are asked upon what grounds they support and base the use of wheat-meal and brown bread, they probably reply that the most nutritious part of the wheat is thrown away when the bran is rejected. Now, really, if one may be allowed to say so, this is all bosh. For this reason: there are several skins covering the nutritive part of the bran, which actually pass through the body undigested. We have in Dr Graham a good authority on this subject. Professor Jago likewise speaks in no uncertain voice upon the fallacy of the brown bread theory.

In a little manual of Grecian antiquities, giving an account of the manners and customs of the ancient Greeks, we have the following extract on bread: 'Bread was their principal food ... the chief attention of the Greeks was confined to wheat bread, and to barley bread. In the composition of the latter they sometimes used oil.'

They did this, no doubt, because they knew no other method either of making the bread or of preparing the grain. The Greeks, highly civilised as they were, had nothing like the knowledge we possess. They did not use machinery at all like ours, even in the most rudimentary state, for properly converting grain into flour. A great many people lose sight of the fact that our milling industry has grown bit by bit from the ancients' crude manner of grinding corn down to the latest improvements of modern times. Why do not the supporters of brown or wheat-meal bread put forward the ancient manner of baking as an argument in support of the same, viz., baking under ashes, on the hearth, or in an earthen or iron pan?

In concluding these brief remarks on brown and wheat-meal bread, I give an abstract from Professor Jago's views on the matter. He says:

> The whole meal and flour from which the bran and germs have not been removed do not keep well. These bodies contain oil and nitrogenous principles which readily decompose, producing rancidity and mustiness in flavour. Not only do the changes occur in the flour, but they also proceed apace in the dough. The diastic bodies of the bran and germ attack the starch, and more or less convert it into dextrine and maltose; they further attack the gluten, that remarkably elastic body which confers on wheaten flour alone of all the cereals the power of forming a light, spongy, well-risen loaf. The gluten, under the action of the bran and germ, loses its elasticity, and becomes fragile and incapable of retaining the gas produced during fermentation: the result is heavy, sodden, indigestible bread.

WHEAT-MEAL BREAD

Granulated wheat meal is superior to rough or whole wheat meal, as it most nearly approaches our modern fine flour.

Dissolve 2½ oz of compressed or German yeast and 2½ oz of salt in one gallon of water of the required heat; make this into a nice dry sponge, and in the morning, or when taken up, add three quarts of water – heated according to the state of the sponge – and 5 oz of salt, and make them lightly into a dough. When it is proved, weigh off for loaves the required size; again prove, and bake. I find from experience that brown flours, of all grades of quality, are best worked up as lightly as possible, and baked with less heat than is necessary for flours of finer quality.

RYE BREAD

is best made from the fine sponge. After breaking-in your sponge in the morning make a bay on the table with as much rye flour as may be required. Put as much of the sponge into the bay as will take up all the flour – or meal, as it is called. Dry it up as well as possible, for it is of a very sticky nature; then proceed in the same manner as for wheat-meal bread.

Rye flour and barley meal flour mixed in equal quantities are sometimes used for the manufacture of rye bread. It is baked in 4-lb, 6-lb and 8-lb loaves. This bread is generally set in the afternoon, so as to be ready to be put in the oven the last thing at night and taken out the first thing in the morning, as a great deal of soaking is required. Put one stone of the above mixture of rye and barley flour into a pan; make a hole in the middle of the flour, and pour into it a good gill of warm water containing 2 oz of German or compressed yeast. Mix a little flour with the liquid, to make a nice soft paste; dust a little flour over the top, and put it in a warm place to ferment. It will not rise much, but will break through the flour on the top: when it is considered ready, put in as much warm water as will take in all the flour, and make into a nice-sized dough. This should be set apart to rise – it should rise to some extent in the dough. Add to the above-mentioned water 2½ oz of salt. When you think the mixture is ready, it may be put into the tins to be proved, and then baked overnight.

BROWN-BREAD MEAL

A well-known baker in the north has lately introduced a brown-bread meal which is a blending of certain cereals. Having worked it, I can safely say it is as near perfection as any of this class. The method of working it is the same as that here given for wheat meal. This particular flour is prepared by Messrs Seatree, of Penrith and Liverpool.

MASLEN BREAD

This bread is very nourishing, and good for those who like it. The bread is made from a mixture of wheat meal and rye meal blended together in equal quantities, and called maslen meal. To every stone of this meal use 4 oz of lard. Place the flour on the table, then make a hole or bay in the centre, and rub the lard with a little of the flour in the centre of the bay. When the sponge that has been set from fine flour has had its quantity of water and salt added and broken in, take as much of the sponge as will use up the full 14 lbs, and place it in the bay or hole made in the flour, making the dough the same size as for ordinary brown bread. Give it the usual time to prove; then weigh off at 1 lb 12 oz for threepence, prove, and bake in a moderate oven. It can either be baked in square tins in the usual manner, or the dough can be placed in oval tins and turned on to a sheet tin, and then proved. This makes the loaf look more fancy, but in using these oval tins, for any kind of bread, and proving and baking by the above method, care should be taken that an air-hole is left in the top of the tin, otherwise the loaf will not rise or appear tradesmanlike when baked. When there is no air-hole in the tin, the likelihood is that the heat of the oven will force the dough out of the bottom of the tin, spoiling what would otherwise be a nice showy loaf. The cause of this is that the steam generated from the moist dough collects in the space between the dough and the upper part of the tin, and when there is no air-hole it naturally forces its way out at the weakest part, carrying the dough along with it. The weakest part in this case is round the bottom rim of the loaf-tin, that is, between the rim and the flat surface of the sheet tin.

AERATED MALT BREAD

This is an excellent bread, which acts both as a tonic and a mild laxative. Weigh 8 lbs of granulated wheat meal, 3 oz of cream of tartar, and 2 oz of carbonate of soda. Sift all these ingredients three times through the sieve, make a bay in the centre of the meal, and add 8 oz of malto-peptone extract, 1¾ oz of salt, and nearly half a gallon of fresh buttermilk. Dissolve the salt and malt extract in the milk, then make into a nice-sized dough. Weigh off at 1¾ lb, mould them oval, and place in dusted oval tins; then turn them on to a large sheet tin, and bake in a sound oven. These are sold at fourpence each.

FERMENTED MALT BREAD

or malt bread made from the morning's sponge after the sponge has had its required salt and water added, and been thoroughly broken in. To every gallon of this sponge use 8 oz of malto-peptone extract (or common malt extract), and 8 oz of lentil flour. Mix all these ingredients together, and then use sufficient granulated wheat meal to make the whole into a nice-sized dough. Let it prove, and work off as for aerated malt bread; then prove them again in the tins. When ready, bake in a sound oven. Weight and price as aerated malt bread.

GERM BREAD

is also a very good bread, taken in conjunction with brown. Dissolve ½ oz of yeast in fully one quart of water, then mix in the water 3½ lbs of germ flour, and let it start fermenting. Put into tins, prove, and bake.

I have been informed that Mr Smith, the patentee of this flour, mixes 8 lbs of salt with every twenty stone of germ flour, therefore no salt need be added.

DIET, OR WHEAT-MEAL BREAD, UNFERMENTED

Take 12 lbs of rough wheat meal, 6 oz of cream of tartar, and 3 oz of soda. Sift these through the sieve, make a bay in the flour, and add 6 oz of castor sugar and 3 oz of salt.

Mix all together with buttermilk, and make into a nice dough, weighing off at 2 lbs for fourpence. Bake on the oven bottom, with oval tins placed over them on the peel. Put into the oven as soon after doughing as possible.

Substitutes for Wheat Bread

Corn, of which bread is made in this and other civilised countries, comprehends the seeds of all ceralia, or farinaceous grass-like plants, for they all contain a farinaceous or mealy substance of a like nature, which substance is chiefly composed of starch. The seeds or grain in common use are firstly and principally wheat, rye, and barley.

Wheat is the only grain from which really good porous or light bread can be made; but rye and barley are occasionally used, as well as other grain. Such bread, however, is of an inferior quality. A sort of bread is made from oats, maize, rice, millet, etc. Rice is said, no doubt truly, to nourish more human beings than all the other seeds which are used for food put together; and it is considered by many to be the most nutritive of all kinds of grain. Accum, in *The Art of Making Bread*, says: 'It has been ascertained that one part of rice contains as much food and useful nourishment as six of wheat.' This, by the way, is an assertion I am much inclined to disbelieve. However, there is no doubt that rice makes a very nourishing, healthy food, notwithstanding the prejudices that prevailed against it on account of the unfounded allegation that it caused eye diseases. Rice is the principal food of eastern nations, a fact that shows that it is not unhealthy. Rice is not often made into bread without flour, and when it is, it forms a loaf of very inferior quality.

Maize is frequently employed as bread-corn in America, but it will not of itself make good loaf bread. Unleavened cakes are made of it, however, which are both nutritive and palatable.

Oatmeal is seldom used for loaf-bread, but it makes an excellent unleavened bread, and is much eaten in Scotland, Lancashire, and several northern counties. It is made into thin cakes called oatcake, and preferred by many to wheaten bread.

BREAD MADE FROM ROOTS

M. Parmentier, at one time chief apothecary in the *Hotel des Invalides*, has published numerous and very curious experiments on the vegetables which in times of scarcity might be used for the support of animals, instead of ordinary food. The result of these experiments, in the mind of M. Parmentier, was that starch is the nutritive part of farinaceous vegetables; and the farina of plants was identical with the starch of wheat. The plants from which he extracted the farina are Bryony, the Iris, the Gladiolus, Ranunculus, Fumaria, Arum, and Dracunculus, the Mandragora, Colchicum, Filipendula, Helleborus, and the roots of the *gramen canum arvense*, or dog grass of the fields. The following is the mode employed by M. Parmentier to extract the starch, or farina from these vegetables: the roots are cleaned and scraped, then bruised and boiled and afterwards reduced to pulp, which being soaked in a considerable quantity of water, deposits a white sediment; this, when properly washed and dried, will be found to be pure starch. M. Parmentier converted this starch into bread by mingling it with an equal quantity of potatoes, reduced to a pulp, and employing the usual quantity of yeast, or other leaven. The bread, I am informed, had no bad taste, and was of excellent quality. From these experiments of M. Parmentier it appears that it is chiefly the amylaceous matter, or starch of grain, that is nutritious; and that the nutritive quality of other vegetable substances depends in a great measure on the quantity of that matter which they contain. Starch formed into a jelly and diffused in water will keep a long time without change.

APPLE BREAD

is a bread said to be very superior to potato bread, and has been made from common apples with meal. Boil one-third of peeled apples; while quite warm bruise them into two-thirds of flour, including the proper quantity of leaven, or yeast; knead without water, the fruit juice being quite sufficient. When this mixture has acquired the consistency of paste, put it into a vessel to rise for about twelve hours. By this process very sweet bread is obtained.

MESLIN BREAD

An excellent bread can be made from what is called meslin. Meslin is a mixture of rye and wheat, raised, or grown, on the same ground at the same time, and reaped, thrashed, ground and dressed in a mixed state.

TURNIP BREAD

is made by mixing turnips in equal quantities with flour. The turnips must be first cleaned, then pared and boiled; wash them and press the water out of them – at least, the greater part; mix with an equal weight of coarse meal flour, and make the dough in the usual manner. When risen, form into loaves, and bake rather longer than for ordinary bread. It will be light and sweet when taken from the oven, with a little taste of the turnip. After being allowed to stand for twelve hours, according to one authority, the taste of the turnip is scarcely perceptible, and the smell is quite gone; after twenty-four hours it would not be known that turnips are in its composition, although it still has a peculiar sweet taste. It appears to be rather superior to bread made of wheat flour only, is fresher and moister, and even after a week continues to be very good. I think, however, it cannot be so good as wheat bread, for, independently of other considerations, turnips do not contain so much starch or nutritive matter as wheat.

SALEP BREAD

Dr Percival recommends the employment of orchis root in powder, or, as it is called, salep. He says that an ounce of salep, dissolved in a quart of water and mixed with two pounds of flour, two ounces of yeast, and eighty grains of salt, produced a remarkably good loaf, weighing 3 lbs 2 oz; while a loaf made of an equal quantity of the other ingredients, without salep, weighed but 2 lbs 12 oz. If the salep be in too great quantities its peculiar taste will be distinguishable in the bread.

OAT AND BARLEY BREAD

The Norwegians, we are informed, make bread of barley and oatmeal grown together. This bread, it is added, improves by age, and may be kept thirty to forty years. At their great festivals they use their oldest bread, and it is not unusual at the baptism of a child to have bread that was baked at the baptism of its grandfather. It is made in extremely thin cakes like oatcake, but much larger, and is baked on a sort of 'back stone', an open flat plate of iron, under which is the fire. It is always made by women.

DEBRETZEN BREAD

In some parts of Hungary, Debretzen for instance, they have a peculiar mode of fermenting bread without yeast, by means of a leaven made as follows: Two large handfuls of hops are boiled in four quarts of water; this decoction is poured upon as much wheaten bran as it will moisten, and 4 lbs or 5 lbs of leaven is added. When the mass is warm the ingredients are well worked together, so as to be thoroughly mixed; it is then deposited in a warm place for twenty-four hours, and afterwards divided into small pieces about the size of hens' eggs, which are dried by being placed upon a board and exposed to dry air, but not to the sun. When dry, they are laid up for use, and may be kept for six months.

BREAD A HUNDRED YEARS OLD

The keeper of the archives for the Hungarian county Marmaros found lately stowed away with some ancient registers a packet bearing this inscription: 'Qualitas panis Marmatici in penuria A.D. 1786.' (Quality of the bread of Marmaros in the year of want 1786.) The bread is partly composed of oatmeal, but the greater portion of it is the bark of trees. I believe the county authorities have directed the specimen to be preserved in the local museum.

Ovens

Among the earliest authentic records we possess of bread ovens are those of the ancient Greeks; and it is a matter for some surprise that they, so far advanced in art, refinement, and culture, should have for any considerable time retained their rude mode of bread baking. If we take into a moment's consideration the beauty of their exquisitely designed porticoes, theatres, forums, and gymnasia – if we think of the temple of Diana of the Ephesians, there is indeed a contrast between their gorgeous splendour and the simplicity of their breadmaking. We are informed that their bread was either baked under ashes or upon the hearth. The most usual mode of baking bread was with an earthen or iron pan, broader below than above, in which the loaves were made. These I believe are the lowest types of ovens on record.

The Romans were without doubt far in advance of the Greeks in this matter; as witness the following passage: 'To the foreign bakers brought to the City were added a number of freedmen, who were formed into a college, or, as we should say, a corporation. From this corporation the bakers were not allowed to withdraw, and their children were by law under the same obligation; and even those who married the daughters of bakers were obliged to become bakers, or members of the bakers' college.' So that it would seem the business of baking was hereditary in Rome. I do not intend to follow up in detail the forms and styles of ovens in vogue among the ancients and in mediaeval times, as it would be of little or no practical use, and would merely weary the reader.

The first oven to be mentioned is the common kitchen oven, placed generally at the side of a fireplace, and having, as a rule, from two to four shelves to hold iron plates. It is fitted with a damper, and is heated by the ordinary fire. These ovens are an absolute necessity to the modern housekeeper, and very few houses are built without them. There are many different kinds, but the one I have described is the one in most general use. There is nothing a good housewife values more than a good, serviceable kitchen oven, as it serves for baking all kinds of bread, dinners, pastry, and all manner of tit-bits. Besides, in cold weather it tends to warm the kitchen, and is thus invaluable to a working man's family.

Iron ovens for baking bread on a large scale are fairly common in some places, but are generally found where brick ovens cannot be introduced. I have seen pastry baked to the very pink of perfection in these ovens. But I would recommend a well-set brick oven for loaf bread. Some of the early forms of bakers' ovens are still to be seen in a few country places at the present day. Those are built round, with the arch about two feet from the bottom, with no damper save the chimney at the oven mouth. There is no chaffer, or furnace ash-hole, or blow-door. The heating is effected by burning wood in the oven. After the requisite heat has been attained, the fire or ashes are raked out with a large iron rake, and the oven is shuffled or mopped preparatory to the baking.

In one place in Cumberland, where the writer called to see an oven of this kind in operation, the batch was in the oven, the door was closed, and the seams and crevices were stopped up with any matter, objectionable or otherwise, that came to hand, to keep, as a woman said, all the steam in. Some of the bread baked in this oven looked excellent.

WAGGON OVENS

Waggon ovens may next be mentioned, or pipe and chaffer ovens, as they are called in some districts. These at one time were in extensive use, chiefly in Edinburgh and Liverpool. They are very dirty to work, entailing a great amount of labour; but for baking bread I consider them very good. A large waggon or chaffer is drawn to the oven mouth by the baker, who after ascertaining that the bars are clear, proceeds to start it. Some dry wood, chopped up to certain sizes, must be lit and placed on the waggon bars: when these are burning, well riddled coals are placed on the top. When this is thoroughly set going, he takes a large iron pipe, from twelve to fourteen feet long, according to the size of the oven, and makes it fast by means of a clasp attached to it, to a catch on the waggon, and then runs the waggon to the further end of the oven. The blow-door is then put up and long strips of paper put over the crevices, if there be any, to accelerate the draught. When the baker thinks it has had sufficient blowing there, he moves the waggon from one side to another, and then into the centre, finishing with the oven mouth. During the process of heating the oven, the waggon must be replenished with coal, and great care is needed to prevent any dust from being among it, for should there be dust present the chances are that the oven draught will blow back with a loud report, covering everything in the bakehouse with soot. When the oven has 'blown down', as the bakers term it, the waggon occupies a recess in the oven side, built for the purpose. Getting the waggon into its place is the most trying thing in working these ovens. A good strong rake is used to push the waggon into the recess; sometimes this is easily done, but at others the trouble caused is past a joke, and the matter is more serious if there is a quick-going sponge. I once worked a waggon oven, thirteen feet long, for over twelve months; but I shall not care if I never work another.

FURNACE OVENS

or flush ovens, as they are sometimes called, will next be treated of. They used to be in great repute on account of their easy management. They range from eight to twelve feet long, and the height from the sole of the oven to the crown of the arch varies from two to three feet. The form of this oven is so common that it would be a waste of time to describe it. It is generally heated with coal, and when well built and when the draught is good, I consider it to be a very useful oven. But where the draught is deficient or the coal of inferior quality, there sometimes are what are called cold corners. If such be the case, no full-flavoured, equally baked, showy loaf can be produced, or the heating of the oven got away with as quickly as is necessary.

SCOTCH OVENS

or Glasgow oven comes next in order. I will try to describe one. Ten feet long by nine feet wide is the most usually adopted size. The sole of the oven is generally laid with quarrels, or tiles; or, which is a better thing, Ayrshire stone, though this is rather expensive. When the sole is being laid I prefer an almost imperceptible rise to be made from the mouth to the back of the oven – about half an inch in ten feet. The oven walls should be at least one foot thick; eighteen inches would be better if the builder is not restricted with regard to price. The height from the sole to the crown of the arch should be no less than three feet six inches. A groined arch is the best and strongest. A chaffer in the right-hand corner is formed in the shape of a half circle; the flue, ten inches square, is at the left-hand corner, running up, slightly slanting, into the chimney, with a damper at a certain distance with which to blow the oven; the door should be no wider than twenty inches, with a flue above containing a check damper. Round the chaffer should be a fender, six inches in height, to keep in the coke; there is, likewise, a blow-door, through which the ashes fall from the chaffer (for this oven is heated with coke), about fourteen inches wide by ten in height. The heating up can be done in the morning in from an hour and a quarter to an hour and a half. If such an oven as I have described does not give perfect satisfaction, none that I know of will.

Before leaving the subject of Scotch ovens, I will give an idea of what one heating will do. First is baked a batch of 2-lb tins, which generally takes three-quarters of an hour. Then come tea cakes, scones, etc.; after which bun loaves (a tea cake dough with fruit in); next Genoa cake, Madeiras, seed cake, and plum; sometimes other varieties. Then the oven is cooled down with a couple of wet shuffles, to bake 360 lbs of gingerbread. This, at a certain season of the year, is what is daily done with one heating of the oven. It must, however, be kept in mind that these ovens bake solid up to the oven-door.

In Belfast, a place that should be designated 'the city of large bakeries,' Messrs Inglis & Co., Limited, have in their bakery a considerable number of Scotch ovens, which enable them to meet the enormous output in that surprising establishment. I may here remark that Messrs Inglis & Co., and their worthy opponent, Mr Bernard Hughes, are proprietors of two of the finest bakeries in the world. Both of these firms are a credit to the baking fraternity, and I hope that they are only pioneers to the goal which the baking trade is at no remote period destined to reach.

VARIOUS OTHER OVENS

are now in general use, amongst which may be mentioned the improved travelling chain ovens; improved gas ovens; Perkin's steam ovens; Mason's ovens, which seem to find general favour; the Bailey baker ovens, now in general use in some districts, and various other decker ovens. I have no doubt that all these ovens have some special merit, and will answer the requirements of certain businesses – such for instance as those where 4 lb or 2 lb loaves are baked exclusively.

There are one-, two-, and three-decker ovens only recently introduced. I have worked a two-decker oven, but – whether from constant use of one-decker ovens, or from prejudice, I cannot say – I do not like them. An oven, which some large firms have adopted, has been put before the public having travelling withdrawable baking plates running on casters, so that the whole bottom of the oven can be filled by hand and run into the oven at the same moment, and drawn out when baked. But from what I learn – only by hearsay – I think they are not much in favour among bakers.

The Climax withdrawable oven is one of the latest constructions in oven building; but I have not seen this new invention in working operation, and therefore do not feel justified in commenting on it.

But I must say that, in my opinion, the oven has yet to be built that can beat the Scotch oven, especially for a mixed trade.

In the working of these ovens no poking or raking is required, nor is there the chance of filling the bakehouse half-full of stifling smoke, which is too often the case in the working of the old style of oven. All that is required is to feed your oven with a certain quantity of coke, keeping your eye on the pyrometer if you have one attached to the oven, and shutting or closing your damper to maintain an even heat of say 520°. If this method be followed, hot and cold ovens will be avoided. The accuracy of my remarks may be proved by testing them in practice.

General Details

THE VENTILATION OF BAKEHOUSES

Fresh air is as necessary to life and health as is wholesome food. At every breath our lungs deprive the air of oxygen, and we breathe out a large quantity of carbonic acid. Now carbonic acid acts as a poison, and discharged breath is, therefore, more or less poisoned air, so that if, instead of inhaling fresh air, we take into the lungs air that has been already breathed, the blood is deprived of the oxygen necessary to enable it to warm and support the body. Therefore through ineffective ventilation, or, which is worse, no ventilation at all, we run the risk of poisoning the blood, and causing disease – the forerunner of death. Physicians declare that such diseases as consumption and scrofula are due far more to poisoned air, inhaled in our houses and factories, than to cold or a changeable climate. If any baker leaves an imperfectly ventilated bakehouse and goes into the fresh air for five minutes, he will, on returning, if gifted with an average amount of intelligence, be shocked at the atmosphere in which he has been living for hours. If the danger mentioned above exists in ordinary houses and workshops, it is not pleasant to think of the condition of dark, underground, badly lighted, and as badly ventilated bakehouses. Like a plant deprived of light, white and stunted in stalk and leaves, so is our poor journeyman baker of pallid, woebegone countenance, because compelled to earn a livelihood in what are little better than fever dens! To work well one must feel well, but under such unfavourable conditions the majority of bakers are unable to do so. Our legislators are to a certain extent to blame for the existence of such a state of things.

THE EFFECT OF COLD OR CHILLED DOUGH ON THE HEAT OF AN OVEN

In large and draughty bakehouses where no heating apparatus is attached, the air of the workshop in cold weather is liable to have a chilling effect on the dough; it likewise has a corresponding effect on the ovens, and must in consequence cool the oven sooner. It is advisable in such bakehouses to have the heat of the ovens a few degrees higher than if they were to be filled with dough not so chilled. To make my meaning clearer, suppose a baker were to run a batch of bread into an oven of, say, 500°F, with the dough at a temperature of 66°F, and then put another batch into another oven of the same heat, with the dough at a temperature of 70°F, the bloom, texture, and flavour of these respective batches could not possibly be the same. A practical man will at once see that this variation in the heat of the dough must, in the natural order of cause and effect, be met by an alteration in the heat of the oven to suit it, so as in some measure, as in the case we have supposed, to equalise their different temperatures. But happily this little wrinkle is very seldom required in a well-appointed modern bakery.

HEATING NEW OVENS

When starting to heat a new oven, the manager of the bakehouse should see that the sole is covered with sawdust, and that the oven is blown up to a gentle heat. Too much heat at first is liable to make the sole expand and the tiles crack, and cause other damage. The sawdust will partly protect the sole till it is a little seasoned. The chaffer should be well filled at night, and the door left open half an inch to allow of the exit of the fuel gas. If the door were shut the gas would put out the fire. Four to six days are required to heat a brick oven.

SEASONING BREAD TINS

All new bread tins ought to be properly seasoned before being used. They require to be put in an oven of an ordinary heat for about one hour. If treated in this manner the tins wear longer, and a better crust can be got on the loaves when baked. When the tins are properly seasoned, the bread they contain requires less time to bake.

HOW TO USE UP OLD BREAD

When a baker finds he has a surplus stock of old bread on hand, the most profitable method of using it up is to make it into bread raspings. It is readily sold at fourpence per pound, to use with fish, hams, soups, and other dainties in the kitchen. The mode of procedure is as follows: Cut the bread into pieces an inch square, and place them into the oven to be well dried. They must be as dry as rusks. When dry, place a quantity on the table and bruise them with a 4 lb weight. With a large rolling or paste pin crush the bruised parts till the whole is of the consistency of fine sand, when it is put away in barrels or boxes for use; or they may be lightly crushed and then ground through a coffee-mill. Sour bread is of no use for raspings on account of its flavour.

HOW TO ASCERTAIN THE HEAT OF WATER

Hold a thermometer in the water and keep moving it gently about for twenty-four seconds; it will then register the exact temperature. This system is more practical than the old style of taking the heat of the water by dipping the hand in it, as by it the baker can work his sponges to a safer and truer degree of exactitude.

A STANDARD FOR BREAD

This would be a novel thing for bakers to adopt. But, as I have said in preceding chapters, progress is the order of the day, and as it is a growing want something of the sort will be adopted. I am not aware that at bread exhibitions there is any particular standard in force for judging the respective merits of bread sent in for competition, general appearance alone being considered. If this is the case it is high time there was something more conclusive, as although a loaf's appearance ought to go a long way in its favour, it is not everything, for the taste should also be taken into consideration. I would suggest the adoption of a standard in which the loaf's merits were considered in something after this order: flavour, texture, colour, moisture, shape, etc. A test like this would stimulate the trade, and help to rouse it from that somewhat happy-go-lucky state into which it has fallen. There are surely men capable enough to assist in the proper consideration of the subject, and to agitate ably enough to secure a successful and creditable issue.

ON CARRYING FLOUR

The time has arrived when this question ought to be settled once and for all. A journeyman baker is neither a Samson nor a Hercules (although I have seen members of our craft who could hold their own in many a well-contested battle); but apart from that, to expect a baker, who perhaps has been at work when other tradesmen have been sleeping, to carry thirty, forty, or it may be fifty sacks of flour, each weighing 280 lbs, is a stigma on the civilising elements of the nineteenth century. All flours should be put up in sacks of 140 lbs, that is, in 10-stone sacks. Journeyman bakers ought themselves to make a move in this matter. It is for those who will follow us, as well as for those now engaged in the trade, that I make this appeal. Future generations of bakers must think that those of the present day were a simple, cowardly lot to have borne the yoke so long. I speak from experience, for I am sorry to say I have seen men carry flour till their shoulders were running with blood. Think of that, ye trade regenerators! Yet this pernicious system is still carried on, more from want of thought than for any pecuniary advantage derived by the millers. However, I see a move has been made in the direction of compelling millers to adopt the ten-stone system. One and all should do their utmost to stop this barbarous practice.

Machinery, Tools, etc.

This is an age of progress, and I think if machinery had not come to the aid of the baker the trade would have been in a sorry plight in this country.

That facilities are wanted now more than in the time of our forefathers the present position of the trade will testify; and my hope is that bakers may meet in a kindly, receptive spirit the various inventions in machinery that are yearly being introduced for their benefit. That great changes of an almost revolutionary character have taken place none will deny. Old systems have been superseded, old plans entirely disregarded, and novel ways and ideas are daily coming into vogue. By contrasting old modes and customs for the making of bread with the modern systems, it will readily be seen that great progress has been made. The old-fashioned method, with the drudgery of its sponging, doughing, and oven work is rapidly passing away, and a method more healthy, cleanly, and expeditious is taking its place. A modern bakery has plenty of room and light, and a thorough system of sanitary arrangements. It has an oven, heat indicator, a flour-testing apparatus, and broad machinery.

The first thing I will touch upon in machinery is the dough-kneading machine, which is one of the greatest boons a baker can have; together with a gas engine. The amount of work performed by a dough-kneader is almost incredible. Before passing from the doughing machine, I would just remark that an inefficient man at the mixer or kneader will go a long way towards spoiling the dough by keeping it too long in the mixer – a thing tending to kill the dough and seriously injure the gluten, which makes the bread dry and flinty.

There is also the dough-dividing machine. I have never worked this, but if it has any of the merits possessed by the bun divider, it cannot fail to be another boon to the trade.

From practical experience I may say that there has not yet been found a proper substitute in the shape of a dough mixer than can compete with hand-made dough; and any bread made by a doughing machine that I have seen comes short in feel and texture to bread made by hand.

Again, there is the flour-sifting machine, which greatly assists in the cleanliness of bread; also the sponge-whisking machine. In the old style of sponge-beating one might be pardoned a muttered malediction on the inventor of sponges when one could scarcely give the whisk another turn. The creaming machine is good in its way, and the peel cutter has prevented many a blistered hand. The currant and sultana washer and drier is another requisite. Thus the old system of making bread is vanishing, deposed by newer and better modes.

PYROMETERS

I would advise any baker intending to build new ovens to get one of these heat indicators, as I find them very convenient in registering the oven's heat. Where they are used the baker has not to work in a haphazard way. But where it is inconvenient to get one, I should advise the baker to procure a special size square-edged tin to hold his coal or coke, and he will soon get to know exactly how much coal or coke is required to obtain the proper heat. Different ovens, flours, and modes of sponging require different heats, but the average is about 500°.

UTENSILS REQUIRED FOR A MODERN BAKERY

It is necessary for a bakery to be supplied with all the latest improvements for producing bread with speed and of good quality. It is worse than foolish for a small firm with only the primitive style of utensils to try to compete with large bakeries. In some cases a man of the old school may, I will not say succeed, but hold his own, by long hours and hard fighting, but no one can prosper without modern plant.

There are some men so prejudiced and narrow-minded in any matters of improvement that they would run the chance of liquidation and the gauntlet of the Bankruptcy Court rather than be suspected of using any novel apparatus, or introducing it into their bakehouses; who will also plainly tell you that what was good enough for their forefathers may serve for them. These men are a drag on civilisation's wheel; they cannot see a week in advance of them; they have no noble instincts to break the bounds of their narrow-minded sphere; men – unworthy of the name – who would consider it a crime to remove the difficulties or soften the sorrows and troubles of their fellow-men. I believe that the introduction of modern education, machinery, and tools, with the healthy information given by our trade journals, will make our craft in the near future second to none. But let me advise the trade journals to try to bury the hatchet of controversy and allow the stream of peace and harmony to run free; then shall we look upon them as the guiding stars of the trade.

Let us then be of one accord in welcoming any useful improvement, noble idea, or better suggestion. We must try to leave the trade in a better condition than we found it, by working for brother tradesmen as well as for ourselves, and instructing and helping one another in order to give it that impetus it so much needs. When chemistry is introduced into our Board schools, and made one of the elements of ordinary education, we shall see with what systematic exactness the manufacture of bread can be conducted.

Of all the requirements of a bakery I think good ovens are the most important. Flour, yeast, tools, in fact nearly everything else can be changed; but when once the ovens are built they remain, as a rule, stationary. So a baker should see that his ovens are the very best that can be built, for on them depend, in a great measure, his chances of success. An oven ten feet long and nine feet broad is quite large enough for successful working, with a pyrometer or heat indicator. Next is the engine, if the bakery is of any size. A gas engine about 2½ horsepower will save a great amount of manual labour. It is likewise more expeditious if there is a trade of anything like fifty or a hundred sacks per week. The gas engine is easily managed, and can be put in motion at a moment's notice. There should always be plenty of hot water at hand; but I do not approve of boilers on the top of chaffers in the oven. Separate boilers are the rule with large firms; so that if barm is used, the water to make it can be had from them. There should also be a cistern for hot and cold water, with a thermometer and a gauge attached. This latter is a handy little article. A doughing or mixing machine, of the most approved pattern, is also wanted. Troughs – or 'trows', as the baker calls them – should be made of clean dry wood, of a handy size, with casters, so that they can be run under the cistern. A good set of barm or quarter tubs is required; and if there is not an office, a writing desk would not be amiss for the convenience of manager or foreman. Then there are the setters, or 'upsets', where batch bread is made, for keeping the loaves from the oven side, etc. They are placed at the sides, back, and front, and are generally of beech, five inches in height and an inch and a half thick. In large firms, a large proving press, of wood, is used in which to put the loaves to prove. It has two doors, and a glass panel to enable the workmen to see within, and is generally heated with a perforated gas pipe bent square or oval. A cistern, lined with zinc, is placed over the gas and partly filled with water, and the press is heated by the steam rising therefrom. A tap is attached to the pipe to control the gas.

A small set of drawers, twelve in number, like a chest, will be found very handy. Each drawer should be made so that it will go in the oven, to be used for proving rolls, baps, scones, etc. Large boards are needed for placing loaves upon when they are rolled up or moulded. Sometimes these are made to fit into the table on slides. Carrying boards are also wanted to put the bread on when drawn from the oven. In large bakeries trucks are used to convey bread to the bread-room. A hand truck is useful for moving sacks of flour. There should be likewise a long rod, or shuffle, with an iron swivel and a ring at the end, to which is attached a piece of net or sacking to clean out the oven. Three or four peels are generally required for each oven – a running peel, very light, with a light mahogany mouth screwed on at the rod end; a drawing peel, heavier and stronger, for drawing out the bread; one for drawing pan bread; and a general peel. The three latter should be made from well-seasoned English elm. A shuffle tub is another thing wanted, also one or two wire sieves, besides a patent flour sifter. Then loaf pans to hold half-quarters, three half-quarters, four half-quarters, two quarters, and three quarters. These sizes are used mostly in Scotland. One-loaf pans are greatly used in England for 4-lb and 2-lb loaves. Flat tins, usually edged all round, about thirty inches long and eighteen broad, are also required; besides sandwich, diet, milk, and Coburg tins; two or three pairs of bakehouse scales; a large flour-weighing machine; barm sieves, butter brushes, wash brushes, table brushes; loaf bread eases; bread stabbers or dockers; weights; a set of oven-bricks for keeping the setters up in front of the batch; a set of water or barm tins; pint, quart, half-gallon and gallon tins; scrapers, or 'scarts', as they are called in Scotland; and a set of good tables to work the bread dough upon. I have seen tables placed in the centre of the bakehouse – the handiest part of the shop – with a quarter-inch iron edging to keep the dough on and the flour from falling off. Two or three large flour scoops are required to feed the doughing-machine; also one or two small scoops; 'clicks', to rake the 'clinkers' off the chaffer; a pedal to feed the chaffer: and a thermometer – not forgetting large sponging tubs for setting quick sponges; dough knives, about the size of a large carver;

sprint boards, floor brushes, etc. A good bakery is also fitted up with a lavatory.

Amongst the latest improvements for a modern bakery is a steam generator for supplying ovens with steam. The contrivance in question is patented by Mr Thoms, and is very highly spoken of; but I am under the impression that a batch of bread, properly manipulated and baked in an oven that is built on the best principles, should generate sufficient steam of itself to satisfy the most critical and fastidious of bakers. The new patent light for ovens should likewise take its place as a sound improvement in helping the ovenman to fill and draw ovens.

Adulteration

ALUM, POTATOES, ETC.

I am indebted to Reid's Guide to the trade for the following. This work is now scarce, being out of print, but in its time it must have been a useful *multum in parvo* to the baking trade.

> Alum and potatoes are now considered indispensable by the London bakers in the manufacture of seconds or household bread, i.e., the bread in daily use in the metropolis. The effect of alum upon bread is not well understood, but it is generally supposed to bleach and act as an astringent. Accum says that the theory of the bleaching properties of alum, as manifested in the panification (making into bread) of an inferior kind of flour, is by no means well understood; and indeed it is really surprising that the effect should be produced by so small a quantity of that substance; two or three ounces of alum being sufficient for a sack of flour.

From experiments in which Mr Reid had been employed, with the assistance of skilful bakers, he was authorised to state that without the addition of alum it does not appear possible to make white, light, and porous bread, such as is used in the metropolis, unless the flour be of the very best quality. Such an assertion as the above, if made to a modern baker who has studied the why and wherefore of fermentation, would be ridiculed.

Mr Reid continues to say:-

Mr A. Booth, the lecturer on chemistry, asserts that alum bleaches from the attraction of alumina, one of its constituents, to the colouring matter of the flour, and also acts as an astringent to the bread.

If these opinions are to be relied upon, of course the question is settled as to the indispensability of alum in making London bread. Accum asserts that he, in conjunction with skilful bakers, has tested the thing by experiments which prove that alum cannot be dispensed with. For my part I am inclined to believe that the whiteness of the London bread is due in some degree to the process of baking – a process widely differing from that followed by women who make home-made bread, which, as I have before asserted, is never so white or so porous as baker's bread, though made of the same flour.

Accum, whatever talent he might possess as a chemist, was a fraudulent writer; and, therefore, his assertions are not to be relied upon. As to the experiments which he alleges he made, I agree with him, however, in his observation that the theory of the bleaching properties of alum, etc., is by no means well understood!

If, as Accum asserts, he had tested the properties of alum in bread, his testing 'apparatus' and 'skilful bakers' must have been of a very low order to allow of such a grave assertion. I have myself tested the properties of alum in bread with modern appliances, and have found the very reverse of what Accum wishes us to believe.

Mr Reid again says:

The quantity of alum used in baking is much less than the public generally imagine, even by the most fraudulent of cheap-bread bakers; and indeed much loss than many of the bakers themselves imagine. This may appear a strange assertion; and it is probably one never made before in print; but a little explanation will make the point quite clear. It is well known that the bakers are liable to a heavy fine if alum is found on their premises. To avoid the liability as much as possible they have been in the habit of buying their alum ready powdered at the druggist's, under the name of 'stuff'.

The druggists keep the 'stuff', which the bakers imagine is unadulterated ground or powdered alum, but which is in reality a compound, consisting of one part of alum to three parts of muriate of soda, i.e., common table salt. This compound is made by pounding the salt with the alum in the mortar. It is kept at the druggist's in pound packages, sold at twopence each.

For this statement I have the authority of several druggists, and the evidence of my own eyes. Extraordinary as it may seem that bakers should allow themselves to be so cheated, I nevertheless believe it to be a fact. It should be recollected that few bakers are readers, and rarely of scientific or medical works.

In the fourth edition of Gray's 'Supplement to the Pharmacopoeia and Treatise on Pharmacology,' under the head of 'Stuff', this term is thus defined:

'Alum, in small crystals, 1 lb, common salt, 3 lbs, to mix with flour for baking.'

I have the evidence of my own senses for the knowledge that respectable bakers of home or household bread do not put more than eight ounces of stuff to a bag of flour; and this 'stuff', on Gray's authority, contains only a quarter, or two ounces, of alum, the remainder being common salt. Some persons, however, ask for powdered alum; but the druggist, knowing from the quantity required and his customer's appearance that it is wanted for baking purposes, invariably serves him with the aforementioned mixture of salt and alum. This I have frequently seen done. The druggist's object is profit. It would scarcely be worth his while to sell powdered alum at twopence a pound. Gray puts it at 1s 6d a pound. This is ridiculously high to sell by the pound, but it is generally sold at a penny an ounce. When the writer gave this information to his baker he exclaimed, 'You don't say so! The infamous rogues! Why, the rascally druggists cheat us before we can cheat our customers!'

Such being the case, it seems almost inconceivable that so small a quantity as two ounces of alum in 280 lbs of flour – the weight of a sack – should have any effect in bleaching, especially when we consider that one hundred parts of alum contain but a fraction over ten parts of alumina, the only constituent in alum, I am informed, that possesses bleaching powers and properties. Nevertheless, there can be no doubt that alum – perhaps not singly, but in conjunction with other ingredients – has the effect of whitening the bread.

A circumstance occurred – I have this on indisputable authority – in the experience of a baker, who by accident left out of his dough the usual quantity of stuff, containing no more than 2 oz of alum. The consequence was a batch of brown bread, necessarily sold at half price.

'There are more thing's in heaven and earth, Horatio, than are dreamt of in your philosophy' – Hamlet.

I have now given the reader Mr Reid's opinion of alum in bread. What his motive could have been in trying to underrate the bad effects of alum I do not know, as Mr Reid was too much of a theoretical tradesman not to have thought differently from what he wrote. But this written opinion will serve another purpose – it shows that at the time of writing the above, adulterating bread with alum was a recognised custom, and much more extensively adopted than he professes.

Herr Van Hamel Ross has recently at Amsterdam detected 30 per cent of marble dust in ground rice imported from Paris. In Haute Vienne one of the most extensive millers of the district has been found to mix carbonate of lead with his flour. This fraud gives the flour a fine appearance, renders it whiter, and enables the dealer to pass off inferior qualities at the price of a better article. The customer is liable, among other misfortunes, to lead poisoning – a trifling consideration to the flourishing, fraudulent manufacturer. Dr Darwin says that when much alum is used it may be distinguished by the eye in the place where two loaves have stuck together in the oven – they break from each other with a much smoother surface than where alum does not exist. I do not recognise this test, having seen batch bread, when drawn from the oven, with a smoothness and texture unsurpassed by any alum-adulterated bread, however skilful in the use of alum a baker may be. The bread referred to was set or sponged with a flying or quick sponge, containing nothing but pure flour, water, yeast, and salt. According to Pownall's work on the 'Assize of Bread', bakers were their own flour manufacturers, and were required by the statutes of assize to manufacture a certain quantity and to sell the bread at a fixed price. But the assize of bread has for a long time been abolished, and the baker now sells his bread for as much as anyone is willing to pay for it. But there is still a heavy penalty demanded from a baker retailing bread short of weight. Potatoes, called by bakers 'fruit', were used at one time for assisting fermentation, and were said to give flavour, and improve the appearance of bread. I do not hold these qualities to be very essential to a baker's success, and he must be very unskilful who cannot produce the qualities desired without resorting to potatoes.

Let us see what the great scientist Liebig says on the subject.

To make bread cheaper it has been proposed to add to dough potato starch or dextrine, rice, the pressed pulp of turnips, pressed raw potatoes, etc. But all these additions only diminish the nutritive value of bread. Potato starch, dextrine, or the pressed pulp of turnips and beet-root, when added to flour yield a mixture the nutritive value of which is equal to the entire potato, or lower still. But no one can consider the change of grain or flour into a food of equal value with potatoes, or rice, an improvement. The true problem is to render the potatoes or rice similar or equal to wheat in their effects, and not vice-versa. It is better under all circumstances to boil the potatoes and eat them as such, than to add potatoes or potato-starch to flour before it is made into bread. This should be strictly prohibited by police regulation, on account of the cheating to which it would inevitably give rise.

Potatoes, however, as well as damaged rice, have been, and no doubt are now used by cheap fraudulent bakers; but I emphatically deny the stories I have heard about bakers using *ground bones* to adulterate bread; and for this reason – the expense of making them fit for such a purpose would be greater than the cost of the flour itself. There are instances on record of bakers being convicted for using gypsum, chalk, and pipe-clay.

Mr Davy, Professor of Chemistry, says that carbonate of magnesia, used in the proportion of twenty to forty grains to one pound of flour, materially improves bread. But, from personal experience, I very much doubt whether any of the obnoxious ingredients mentioned help in any way to improve the appearance or the flavour of a loaf of bread. I must in all fairness say that, so far as I can learn, there never has been a time in the history of the baking trade when the consumer has been better protected, or a better class of bread has been put before the public, than the present. We may in a great measure thank the Food Adulteration Act for this; but I only give the baker his due in expressing the belief that education, with its civilising effect, has more to do with the present state of affairs than laws passed in order to keep him in the path of honesty.

A baker occupies a post of more responsibility than the generality of the public give him credit for. For instance, when a person fed on bread of a sour, heavy, sodden, unpalatable nature is compared with one in the same condition of life, fed on good, light, porous bread, of a fine nutty flavour, common sense will indicate which of them enjoys life best, or thinks it best worth living, when the chances of taking an active part in life, and of building up a strong, robust constitution, are so unequal. I think, therefore, the public ought to be a little more compassionate to the poor journeyman baker, whose lot is by no means one of the pleasantest in the world.

Appendix

BAKING AND BAKERS IN THE TIME OF THE ROMANS

Associated as bakers are with a necessary article of food in daily use, of which we are never satiated, as in the case of other food, bread itself is surrounded with a wealth of history; from its origin, so crude, to the varieties of later times; concerning the forms in which it was made; the reverence in which it was held; the abundance, and the want of it, with the substitutes used to satisfy the craving for it, or made use of by less civilised people in days gone past. I will in the first place try to show bakers what their position has been, especially in the time of the Romans.

In 1834 the Society for the Diffusion of Useful Knowledge published two volumes of a work entitled 'Pompeii'. This work is of great interest to the baker, as it lifts the veil from the hidden past and reveals to him what, but for the destruction of Pompeii, would never have been known, viz., some of the customs and usages of the baking trade 1800 years ago. Until I read this work I had no idea that the baker was provided with a goddess, Fornax, the goddess of the oven. It goes on to say that the Romans were very careless of the amount of labour wasted in preparing an article of daily and universal consumption. This probably arose chiefly from the employment of slaves, the hardness of whose tasks none cared about; while the profit and encouragement to enterprise on the part of the baker was proportionately diminished, since every wealthy family prepared its bread at home.

But the same inattention to the useful arts pervaded all they did. Their skill in working metals was equal to ours. Nothing can be more beautiful than the execution of tripods, lamps, and vases; nothing coarser than their locks – at the same time the door handles, bolts, etc., which were placed where they would be seen, were often exquisitely wrought. But the demands of a luxurious nobility would never have repaid any man for devoting his attention to the improvement of mills – (I here refer to the hand mills the Roman bakers had for grinding their corn) – and there was little general commerce to set their ingenuity to work.

Originally, mills were turned by hand, and this severe labour seems, in all half-savage times, to have been conducted by women. It was so in Egypt (see Exod. xi. 5); it was so in Greece in the time of Homer, who employed fifty females in the house of Alcinous upon this service; it was so in Palestine in the time of the Evangelists; and in England in the 14th and 16th centuries. Harrison, the historian, two centuries later, says that his wife ground her malt at home upon her quern. Those who had been guilty of an offence were sent to the mill as a punishment, and sometimes forced to work in chains.

The oven of the Roman baker was made with considerable attention to economy of heat. The real oven was enclosed in a sort of ante-oven, the latter having an aperture in the top for the smoke to escape, and a hole in the side for the introduction of dough, which was prepared in an adjoining room, and deposited through that hole on a shovel. The bread when baked was placed in a room on the other side of the oven, through a similar aperture, to cool. For a long time bakers used their corn sodden into pap; and there were no bakers in Rome before the war against Pyrrhus, King of Macedonia (Pliny, xviii.) about AD 580. Before this, every house made its own bread, and even after the invention of bread, it was long before mills were known. Their loaves appear to have been very often baked in moulds, several of which have been found. They may possibly be *artopae*, and the loaves *artopicii*. Several of these loaves have been discovered; they are flat, and about eight inches in diameter. One in the Neapolitan has a stamp on the top.

Thus we have here a description of both ovens and bread, 1800 years ago. If Britain be destined to relapse into such a state of barbarism as Italy passed through in the period which divides ancient and modern history, its inhabitants a thousand years hence will know, we hope, a little more of the manual process of breadbaking in our time, than we do of the ancient Roman baking trade.

Three bakers' shops have been discovered in a tolerable state of preservation in Pompeii; the mills, the oven, kneading troughs, vessels for containing water, as well as flour and leaven being also found. One of these shops was attached to the house of Sallust; another to the house of Pansa, and these were no doubt worth a very handsome rent to the proprietors.

In every Roman bakehouse there was a chief, or master, called *patronus*. This person had the superintendence of the bakehouse and the ordering of all matters therein. These patrons elected every year one out of their number who had the care of the college and the scrutiny of the general body. That bakers were highly respected by the Romans is proved by the fact that, although as individuals they could own no property, yet now and then one became a senator. And indeed in every nation the first bakers were highly respected. Whether this arose from the eating of good fermented bread instead of hard unleavened cake, it is hard to determine. Pharoah's chief baker, it is plain, was regarded by his master as one of the most important men in Egypt, from the fact that he was consulted upon a matter affecting the personal comfort of the monarch.

By the statutes of England bakers are considered superior to those employed in handicrafts. 'No man' – according to 22nd Henry VIII, cap. 13 – 'for using the mysteries of the science of baking, brewing, surveying, or writing shall be interpreted a handicraftsman.' Thus it appears that bakers, like writers – now called attorneys – are gentlemen by Act of Parliament; but it is a remarkable fact that no baker has ever risen to the honour of the Lord Mayoralty of the City of London.

However, to return to the Romans. The ancient bakers had hand-mills near their ovens; these were originally nothing more than pestles and mortars with which they reduced corn to flour. Let the reader pause for a moment, if he be a baker, and contrast this slow system of grinding with the expensive and elaborate machinery now in use. What a great change from the customs of the misty past! The bakers were called in Latin (as were the millers previous to the introduction of baking as a profession), *pistores*, or pounders. For the same reason the Roman bakehouses were called *pistoria*. The Roman college or incorporation of bakers had granted to them all the mill utensils, slaves, animals, and everything, in short, that

belonged to the *pistoria*. In addition to these the corporation
received considerable land, and nothing was withheld that
could assist them in pursuing their trade or profession to the
best advantage. It appears that the more laborious part of the
business, such as grinding the corn, etc., was not performed
by the bakers themselves, as persons found guilty of petty
offences were condemned to work for a certain period in the
bakehouses, and even the judges of Africa were obliged every
five years to send to Rome such criminals as had incurred that
kind of punishment. The bakehouses, of which in the time of
Augustus there were no less than 329, were distributed over
the fourteen divisions of the city, and no baker could pass from
one bakehouse to another without special permission; they
were not permitted to attend gladiatorial shows, much less to
become gladiators themselves, nor to be connected with the
comedians. To the care of the Roman bakers the public granaries
were committed; they paid nothing for the corn used in baking
bread that was to be given to the poor citizens, and the price of
that intended to be sold was regulated by the magistrates. No
corn was given out of these granaries except for the use of the
bakehouses or for that of the emperor, and it is recorded that
if any baker were convicted of having converted any part of
the grain belonging to the public granaries to his own or any
improper use, he was made to pay a fine of 500 lbs of gold –
so enormous a sum of money that we cannot help doubting
the truth of the statement. It is also recorded that when the
Gauls sought to subjugate Rome, the god Jupiter suggested a
novel mode of defending the city – namely, pounding their
assailants with loaves of bread! and I believe that they were so
well pounded with such a host of these strange weapons that

the besiegers, who had relied on starving out the Romans, shortly withdrew. We are told that the younger Gracchus, for the sake of popularity, compelled the state to sell corn at a loss to all Roman citizens.

Our Saxon ancestors knew but little about bread. In the days of Queen Elizabeth the bread at meal times was handed round on the point of a sharp knife. It is but a short step from good Queen Bess to James I. The art of cookery, instead of advancing, must have fallen to a low ebb in this reign, as I believe the feasting was of barbarous kind, and the dishes prepared were of a questionable nature. In 1661, at a feast, four huge pigs were served, harnessed and bitted, with strings of sausages attached to a monstrous hag pudding. Snails, frogs, and curiosities dished up and made palatable were the fit accompaniments of the riotous feasting that set in, the expenses of which for one year in the Royal household amounted to the respectable figure of £100,000; not a bad sum in those times for the treasury to meet. It is also recorded that Charles II was very fond of specially prepared gingerbread, but my opinion is that this king and his court, according to history, required something more substantial than common gingerbread to satiate their discriminating appetites.

From the time of King Charles to that of Queen Victoria, nothing occurred to elevate or develop our trade, which, still harassed with old superstitions and customs, struggled in mists it could not dispel till the year 1845 June 26th, when the Repeal of the Corn Laws was secured. Then the baking trade commenced to draw itself together; a few inquiring minds came to the front; and the baking trade awoke to new life. From that time to the present what stupendous improvements have been made in the plant of a bakery! Sponging is still left to us as an incubus, and seems to baffle the most learned, scientific, and foremost men of our time; but that a barm, or yeast, will by and by be produced to meet the requirements of the age I do not for a moment doubt. When yeast, or barm, was first used for the purpose of raising dough I have no reliable information; it seems hidden in past ages.

JOURNEYMAN BAKERS IN LONDON

All things have rest; why should we toil alone; We only toil who are the first of things,
And make perpetual moan.
Still from one labour to another thrown,
Nor even fold our wings
Nor cease from wanderings. – *Tennyson.*

The journeyman baker begins work at eleven o'clock at night, and after a night's work of a most laborious nature, he starts with the ferment. At six in the morning he mixes his ferment, and re-heats the oven a little for the rolls, cottage bread, etc., which are made from part of the common bread dough set aside for the purpose, its superior lightness being due to a longer proving. While the rolls and cottage loaves are baking, he carries the bread just baked into the shop, and then cleans out the bakehouse – that is, he washes the seasoning tubs, scrapes out the troughs, and cleans up generally. The rolls by this time are about ready to draw from the oven and be sent to the shop. He next takes his breakfast in the bakehouse, and when all is done and everything ready the bakings for the public begin to come in. This will occupy him till about one o'clock; the poor man now gets his dinner; from two till four he is out serving customers; about five he sets his sponge, and then washes down his hand van. It is now well on for six o'clock, when he is supposed to go to bed and sleep till eleven, at which time his sponge will be ready. After he has made the dough and set away the ovens, he will have an hour's sleep. By this time his dough is ready to throw out upon the table; he then weighs off, moulds, and sets the batch, as it is called in London. Now he may have another sleep, and then comes the drawing of the batch, etc. This is considered an easy place! and a man has to have a good character to get it. On Saturday night I have seen men at work up to ten o'clock, and then have to be in the bakehouse early on Sunday morning, to prepare the ovens for Sunday's baking. All this, too, is done in an unhealthy atmosphere in a confined cellar. This is known as a single-handed place; the man is called a Scotch foreman. There are better places than this in London, but they are the exception. This system is carried on daily in the most civilised city in the world, and the wages paid for such slavery are from £1 to 26s per week – surely not sufficient to keep a man honest. Were the London bakers better paid, and had they to work more Christianlike hours, we should hear less about London bakers being convicted for making 'dead uns', or 'dead men' – charging a credit customer for six loaves, for instance, when they only deliver four. Some of my readers may think that I am overpainting this horrid state of things. But let me mention as a fact that it has been officially stated, as recently as the month of January, 1891, at a coroner's inquest held in the east end of

London, on the body of a baker's child who literally died from starvation, that the father of the child was working seventeen and eighteen hours per day for the mere pittance of three shillings and sixpence per week. What has come over Britain's boasted Christianity and philanthropy when we find ourselves among facts like these? Well may bakers quote Burns's poem, 'Man was made to mourn'. One verse is very appropriate in their case:

> Oh, Death I the poor man's dearest friend –
> The kindest and the best!
> Welcome the hour my aged limbs
> Are laid with thee at rest!
> The great, the wealthy, fear thy blow,
> From pomp and pleasure torn!
> But oh! a blest relief to those That weary-laden mourn!

OLD CUSTOMS OF THE TRADE

There is an old saying that old customs die hard; but there are one or two customs we would like to give more longevity to than they are likely to have, viz., the yearly reunions of the trade; such as balls, suppers, and excursions, or, as they are called in London, 'Bean Feasts'. I can well remember my debut at a ball. As officer, that is, the oldest apprentice at the trade who had not held the office before, I was presented with a free ticket; the duties were not very onerous – just to deliver summonses, attend meetings, etc. At that particular ball, I can well remember many master bakers and master millers (as the millers and sugar boilers were counted with our craft), and how sociably the employers mixed with the employed; for a few weeks before, and a few weeks after, it helped to brighten the lives of the bakers, both young and old. The usual thing was for a young man to select a suitable partner, one who could dance of course; and on presenting her with a ticket, it was customary to present her with a pair of gloves, or the equivalent, say, from 5s to 10s according to his position. When the ball night (generally early in the new year) arrived, he would take a cab and call for his partner. Arrived safely, he would conduct her to the cloakroom, and next to the ball-room, where the ladies sat on one side and the gentlemen on the other. When all the guests arrived a slight refreshment would be served round. I have been one of the stewards, and it was pleasant to carry round a tray of eatables, or wine, etc., and chat with the ladies. Then the band would strike up the Grand March, and each baker and his partner walked round the room, the ball committee going in front. We always broke up the proceedings with regret, at about five o'clock in the morning; escorted our partners home, changed, and started our day's work and duties again. Bakers' suppers have given place to balls, and they seem to be dying out. I am alluding principally to provincial towns. The bakers used to club together to the tune of thirty or forty – though I have seen fewer. It used to be two shillings and sixpence per head; and subscriptions or collections were taken for the waiters or waitresses, and as a rule they used to fare very well. After all had gathered a chairman and vice-chairman were selected; then the landlord or lady was desired to bring in the good things provided for us – for the supper was usually held in an hotel. After someone had been asked to pronounce a blessing, the fun of the evening began. Ample justice being done to the viands, everything was cleared away, and refreshments came in the shape of cigars, pipes, and ale and whiskey, and the evening was enlivened with songs, recitations, etc., so that in an hour or two we could say with Burns – with a slight alteration – 'Kings may be blest, but the bakers were glorious'. The hotel proprietors were sometimes granted an extra hour, and the party broke up singing 'Auld Lang Syne'. At one of these reunions there was a baker, an old man, but one of the right sort, who could tell a good story and was generally put down for two or three songs after the supper – which songs always had a chorus, in which we all joined and made the rafters sound! They were mostly trade songs, and his refrains usually ran after this fashion:

Every man to me'e a brother That wears flour upon his coat.

Or,

Bakers get enough to vex them,
Whiles wi' barm, an' whiles wi' flour.

The poor old man lived to a ripe old age, but has by this time crossed the bourn, and has known the grand Secret for some years.

Excursions are mostly the fashion now; and, of course, they will run till, as other fads are adopted, they become things of the past.

There used to be old customs of initiating a new apprentice into the mysteries of the trade. One was to get a new apprentice to go to a neighbouring bakery with an empty sack and ask for the loan of their crystal chaffer. When the boy arrived with his request he was asked to leave his sack and call in a few minutes, which he invariably did. In his absence all the available bricks and ashes were put into the sack, and a load made ready for him sufficient for a donkey to carry. When he arrived the crystal chaffer was lifted on to his back with strict injunctions not to let it fall, and the poor fellow had to manage as well as he could. But he was not likely to forget that journey, nor the laughter that greeted him on his return.

Another custom was to send a boy with a large pail for a pennyworth of pie-barm. He was, of course, asked to leave the pail, and bricks were put into the bottom of it, and it was filled up with water to the brim, with just a sprinkling of flour on the top. He was told not to spill any, as it was valuable and scarce. He generally managed to take it to the bakehouse, where the men laughed 'fit to split' at his wrestling exertions to keep it from spilling.

Some eighteen months ago a new boy was engaged in our establishment, and in the first week I noticed on a particular day some of the men coming down the bakehouse stairs laughing, and others trying to suppress their mirth. I went upstairs to ascertain the cause, and on going into a certain place where the muffin stove is kept, whom should I see but the new apprentice trying to keep his hands in a tin of boiling fat, with the perspiration running down his face, and his body trembling all over. I asked him what was the matter. 'I am boiling my hands, sir,' said he, 'so that the dough may not stick. If you please, sir, will you look at them and see if they will do?' The poor boy's hands were in a bad state, and I gave an affirmative decision; but, though sorry for him, I nearly hurt myself with laughter, as though I had often heard of it I had never seen the trick played before.

Another old custom, but one which is rapidly becoming extinct, owing to the adoption of Parisian and other barms, was hunting for 'skeechan' on a Sunday morning. (This term must have been peculiar to the trade in certain districts, as I cannot find it in Jamieson's Scottish Dictionary. I have therefore given it so as to represent as nearly as possible the pronunciation common in the trade.) Not so many years ago Company's barm was used in many parts of Scotland, the chief seat of its manufacture being Edinburgh and Leith. This barm in its constituent parts resembles brewers' barm, and was used in ferments much in the same way. There was a liquid that settled on the top of the barm, which was, compared to ale, what methylated spirit is to whiskey. This was the 'skeechan'. After a Saturday night's debauch, when the funds were low, it was a common custom for bakers to watch the time that the foreman went to set his ferment, so as to get a pint or two of this hateful concoction. Their modus operandi was to warm the liquid and sweeten it with sugar; and I have heard keen expressions of delight and approval from the partakers of this detestable beverage. But the majority of these poor, infatuated fellow-workmen gradually descended in their social position, till they reached that unenviable part of the community, the 'submerged tenth'. This old custom is, let us hope, a thing of the past.

Just another custom that used to exist in Scotland. At New Year's time a great quantity of shortbread was baked for the coming festivities, and the apprentice was allowed the scrapings. The shortbread, be it remarked, was scraped on the bottom before being sent into the shop. The apprentice was generally equal to the occasion, and made it known outside that he had shortbread scrapings for sale, a big handful for a half-penny. If trade was good, and the demand bade fair to be more than the supply, he used to mix bread raspings with the scrapings, which were often adulterated to such an extent as to spoil the custom.

A CANNY SCOT

It is surprising and amusing to learn what ignorance was displayed by bakers at no very distant date in regard to the practical knowledge of working sponges. I could enumerate many instances, but this will suffice: – In a small town in Scotland a baker had just finished setting his ferment, when he heard the sound of a horse and cart coming into the street. He was afraid that the rattling of the cart would injure his ferment, and was greatly annoyed; so calling to the boy, said – 'Bin awa, laddie, an' tell that chiel tae be canny wi' his cart; I hae jist gat the ferment set.' This individual would stare if he was brought into some of our modern bakeries, where there are ferments, quarter sponges, etc., all in different stages of operation, and machinery rattling loudly enough, one would think, to shake this Rip Van Winkle out of his bed.

SCIENTIFIC VIEWS ON FERMENTATIVE PHYSIOLOGY

In order to further enhance the value of this work, and to keep the trade well to the front on this important subject,

I have here introduced the opinions of a few leading British and Continental scientists on fermentation and fermentative physiology.

In an article on 'Yeast – Its Morphology and Culture', A. Gordon Salamon, ARSM, FJC, FCS, says:

It remains, therefore, to decide as to whether it is an animal or a plant. In this we are again assisted by reference to the typical conditions pertaining to the life of both. Now microscopic examination of a yeast cell shows that it is surrounded by an envelope or sac of cellulose, and although there may be variations in the thickness of this envelope, there is reason to believe that it is continuous; in other words, that it does not exhibit orifices such as exist in animals for the introduction of food within the system, and for the excretion of products voided as the result of food assimilation; and further, since the single cell is capable of life and reproduction, it follows that the continuous cell wall and the contents which it encloses must constitute the whole machinery which is enabled to manifest these phenomena.

In the case of nearly all animals the food is conveyed into the system by means of an opening adapted to the purpose. Now with the yeast cell such a means of introduction is impossible, because of the existence of the continuous cell wall, which is unprovided with openings; and if the cellulose wall were broken, the life of the cell would be determined. It is therefore clear that the only way in which food can be conveyed into the interior of the cell is by passage through the cellulose. This is, indeed, what actually happens, and it is accomplished by means of diffusion or osmosis. We shall inquire further into the nature of this process at a later stage; for the present it will suffice to state that one of the conditions essential to diffusion through cellulose is that the substance diffused must be in a state of solution; hence it follows that no food can be assimilated by yeast unless it is previously dissolved.

These facts tend to prove that yeast is a plant, because a cellulose wall, and the passage of dissolved nutrient matter through it by osmosis, constitute two of the most essential conditions of plant life. But the conclusion is greatly strengthened, indeed corroborated, by other considerations dependent upon the chemical constitution of the food assimilated. Now animals and plants have this in common; apart from certain mineral elements, which, for the moment, we can ignore, they both require a supply, in some form or other, of the elements carbon, hydrogen, oxygen, and nitrogen. So, as far as information goes, these elements must be aggregated as certain molecular combinations before they can be regarded as nutrifying ingredients.

Among these combinations we recognise a group of complex nitrogenous bodies known as proteins. Their supply would seem to be essential to a normal, healthy, and continued existence both of animals and plants. Suitable animal food contains these protein bodies ready formed in a state available for assimilation, and proportioned in quantity to the climatic conditions and life history of the organisms by which they are consumed. If the animal did not find the protein nourishment ready made it would not be competent for it to manufacture it or build it up out of the elements of which it is composed. For instance, protein bodies are strictly organic compounds as distinguished from minerals, and it would not be possible for any animal to form protein out of mineral matters. This is not so with plants. They are possessed of the property of forming or manufacturing it from the elements or from true mineral substances, which latter they have the power of breaking down or decomposing in order that the requisite elements may be devoted to the purpose. This is found to hold good with all plants, but with no animals; and it therefore establishes a fundamental difference between the two which is sufficient to constitute a reliable test in case of doubt. Applying it in our own case, we find that yeast is possessed of this power of forming protein out of mineral substances. The point has been abundantly proved by Pasteur. He showed how millions of cells, each containing its requisite amount of protein, could be produced in a healthy and thriving state from a smaller number of parent cells by introducing the latter into a fluid of the following definite composition: Water, sugar, ammonic tartrate, potassium phosphate, calcium phosphate, magnesium sulphate.

The growth of yeast in this fluid is accompanied by the gradual disappearance of the above-named constituents, and the formation in all the newly developed yeast cells of protein bodies. The latter were obviously not present in the original fluid. It can be proved that the mineral substances present have not the power of forming them in the absence of the yeast or some other similarly constituted organism, and hence it follows that in this case they must have been formed by the yeast, and at the expense of the original constituents of the fluid. Moreover, the recent researches of Hansen have shown that the same results could have been produced by introducing a single cell into the fluid instead of several or many, as was done by Pasteur.

Another high authority, William Jago, FCS, FIC, in the journal of the Society of Chemical Industry, thus treats on 'Fermentation in its Relation to Bread Making':

Fermentation has been made the subject of careful and systematic study in connection with brewing and the production of alcoholic liquors generally; but in its relation to breadmaking has hitherto received but comparatively little attention from scientists. In many cases it has apparently been assumed that yeast behaves in just the same manner in dough as it does in a malt or other wort, and, consequently, that the same laws apply with equal force to the phenomena of fermentation in either substance. But the fermentation of wort differs from that of dough in several most important particulars. The former is a liquid, rich in maltose, and well adapted for the sustenance and growth of yeast; the latter is a stiff, elastic, semi-solid mass, containing but little readily fermentable matter. In wort, by a process of budding, yeast rapidly multiplies; but when added to dough the yeast cells show no signs of any reproduction by budding, but, on the contrary, gradually disappear, owing to the breaking down of the cell-walls. In the fermentation of wort but a small proportion of the effect is due to the yeast originally added, the greater part being produced by the new yeast cells formed as the progeny of those first introduced; but in dough the whole of the work is thrown on the yeast cells primarily introduced into the mass. These are so unfavourably situated as to have little or no power of reproduction, and consequently on their activity and vitality successful fermentation must depend. This being the case, it is evident that mature and vigorous yeast is more absolutely essential to the baker than even to the brewer; since, if the latter's initial fermentation be sluggish, the progeny of new cells may fairly be expected to be more active. On the other hand, absolute freedom from foreign ferments is not a point of such vital importance to the baker as to the brewer. In many cases, a yeast that on microscopic examination would be immediately rejected by the brewer, would be found capable of making good bread. I might even go a step further and say that of two yeasts the one deemed the better of the two, judging by purity as revealed by the microscope, might be the less desirable yeast for bread-making purposes. It is a well-recognised fact that in some varieties of bakers' barms the presence of other organisms than the yeast plant is normal. In particular, this is so with Scotch flour barms, which consist of yeast allowed to develop in what is essentially a thin paste made from scalded flour. This barm invariably contains the lactic ferment in large numbers.

Theory and practice both show that the aeration of the dough is only one out of several important effects produced by fermentation. From time to time, those interested in other methods of bread manufacture insist on the great loss caused by fermentation; thus, Dauglish expressed the opinion that this loss amounted to from 8 to 6 per cent, which opinion has since been adopted by Dr Richardson in his work on the 'Healthy Manufacture of Bread'. In order to determine the maximum amount of loss possible, I recently made the following experiment: 100 parts by weight of soft flour from English wheats were made into a slack dough with distilled water, two parts of pressed yeast being added, and no salt used. This dough was allowed to stand for from eight to nine hours at a temperature of about 85° to 90°F.; fermentation proceeded violently, but towards the end of the time had apparently ceased. The dough was next placed in the hot-water oven, and dried until of constant weight; the same weight of flour and yeast, unmixed, and without water, was also placed in the oven. At the end of the time, the fermented dough was found to have lost 2.5 per cent, compared with the flour. In this extreme case, a soft flour was used with distilled water and no salt, and about six times the normal amount of yeast; the temperature was purposely maintained at a high point, and the fermentation carried on so long as any decided evolution of gas occurred. Yet, under those conditions, which far and away exceed in severity any such as occur in practice, the loss was less than Dauglish's minimum estimate. The percentage of loss closely corresponds with that of sugar in flour as determined in a series of experiments to which I wish to direct your attention. Mr Williams, a practical baker of high authority, estimates, from a series of experiments he conducted on a large scale, that the loss of solid constituents of flour during fermentation, as practically conducted in bakeries, amounts to 1.37 per cent.

Mr Thoms, FRMS, a Scotch master-baker, who has for very many years investigated yeast most exhaustively from the baker's standpoint, is the authority for the following. He says:

On brewing flour-barm at a sufficiently low temperature to prevent the development of *Bacterium Lactis*, the barm produced is inferior in quality and yields an inferior loaf. It should be added that in bread made on the Scotch system there is always a distinct, though very slight acid flavour; this acidity is altogether different in character from what is known as sourness in bread in the London district. The flavour of Scotch bread more resembles that wetted partly with buttermilk. With healthy, active yeast cells, fermentation, as conducted in the south, proceeds sufficiently rapidly in dough to allow the bread to be completely ready for the oven before the lactic ferments have had time to develop any sensible acidity. In deciding as to the quality of yeast for breadmaking purposes the first requisite is that the yeast plant itself should be in a vigorous and active condition. Among foreign ferments the presence of those producing lactic, at least, is not deleterious in small numbers to anything like the extent that holds in the case of yeast to be used for beer brewing. Apart from their own specific action, foreign ferments are, in brewer's yeast, an evidence of carelessness and want of strict cleanliness in the yeast manufacture, and to this extent their presence may be interpreted unfavourably when judging the value of such a yeast for the baker. The thing I hope I have made clear is, that if the yeast itself is healthy and vigorous, foreign ferments are not capable of doing the same amount of harm during the fermentation of dough, as during that of beer, principally because the act of baking the bread effectually destroys all fermentative action before disease ferments have had time to set up any injurious chemical change. In passing, the aim of the baker in availing himself of the action of the yeast during breadmaking may be explained. If the question were asked, 'Why is yeast employed?' the answer in ninety-nine cases out of a hundred would be – 'To aerate the dough, and thus make the bread spongy.' Now yeast possesses this property in common with various other substances. There are, in fact, several ways of aerating bread more or less satisfactorily, but fermentation seems to be the only method capable of inducing other changes which are essential to the production of bread of the finest quality. By the action of yeast, the gluten, which contains the principal nitrogenous constituents of flour, is softened and mellowed, undergoing a species of digestive action, partly physical, inasmuch as it is rendered softer; and probably partly chemical, as a change analogous to peptonisation apparently occurs. Another most interesting effect of fermentation is that it imparts a characteristic and pleasant flavour to bread absolutely unattainable by other means. In bread aerated by any other method, the result of these specific changes is absent; and public opinion decides that, after a time, such bread raised otherwise than by the action of yeast has a raw uncooked taste, of which the palate speedily tires. Although the average baker knows nothing of the nature of the chemical changes induced by yeast, it is of great interest to note that his methods take cognisance of the fact that such changes are produced. If the production of sufficient gas to aerate the dough were his only object, then it might be expected that as soon as that object was attained, he would proceed to get his bread in the oven. Such, however, is not the case. After a time, as much as possible of the gas generated in the dough is violently knocked out of it, this operation being sometimes repeated two or three times. The baker knows by experience that other changes which he desires to have take place, will not be completed until some time after sufficient gas to aerate the bread has been developed. Theory and practice, therefore, both show that the aeration of the dough is only one out of several important effects produced by fermentation.

Dr Emil Chr. Hansen, in a series of papers on 'Practical Researches in Fermentation', thus gives the practical results obtained by the use of pure cultivated yeasts – of which he was one of the first advocates:–

When, in 1883, I asked permission of the late Captain Jacobsen to try my system on a large scale at his brewery at 'Old Carlsberg,' he did not give me much encouragement. One of his principal objections was that a pure cultivated yeast would not ensure proper after-fermentations, to which an admixture of wild types was probably essential. Shortly before I had obtained some remarkable practical results, tending strongly to confirm the correctness of my views of saccharomycetes. In a paper on 'Diseases of Beer' (1883), I explained the affection which for two years past had proved so troublesome at the Tuborg brewery, near Copenhagen – i.e., yeast-turbidity, and as application of my conclusions had speedily put matters right, manifest proof was afforded of the practical worth of my discoveries. About the same time Jacobsen experienced a difficulty in his own brewery, where the beer had acquired a bitter twang and a bad smell. According to the then prevailing idea, this was attributed to bacterial infection, and when this could not be detected, the blame was laid on the wort and more particularly on the hops. Here, likewise, nothing could be detected. Previously, in 1882, I had published an account of an experiment with one of the saccharomycetes, which gave a beer similar to that complained of at Old Carlsberg.

I also mooted the idea that wild yeasts do as much mischief in various departments of fermentative industry as bacteria. In 1883 I advanced a step further. My success at Tuborg afforded me the desired opportunity. This experiment was carried out in actual brewing practice, on a large scale, and the proofs obtained step by step were irrefragable. From an impure yeast I separated four different types of saccharomycetes, and after experimenting with them singly and in admixture, found that only one of them gave normal beer of good flavour and smell. Among the others I found the type I had employed in my experiment of 1882, and of which I gave a description in 1883, under its present name of *Saccharomyces pastorianus I*. This alone produced the affections in question. Further, I found that whilst beer produced with the suitable type of yeast alone was excellent, the admixture of *Saccharomyces pastorianus I* therewith gave the dreaded bitter taste and disagreeable smell. This result proved of great importance. Jacobsen saw that reform was practically within reach, and threw open his whole establishment for the purpose. A beginning thus made, matters progressed as rapidly as ever I could desire. That was in 1884. I have mentioned the results obtained in the two breweries just named, partly to show the progressive development of the idea, partly as affording tangible proofs in favour of a reform which I desired to see spread as widely as possible. Proof was likewise afforded that Jacobsen's fears respecting after-fermentation were groundless. Nevertheless, the doubt has since been raised in other quarters (see Brown and Morris's paper on 'The Non-Crystallisable Products of the Action of Diastase on Starch' in Journal of the Chem. Soc., 1885.) Among English experimenters only, I have met with the objection that the highly alcoholic English top-fermentation beers present special difficulties in the way of employing pure cultures. In Danish top-fermentation breweries, where less alcoholic beers are produced without special after-fermentations, A. Jorgensen has since 1884 employed the method, slightly modified, with satisfactory results, and in accordance with his verbal explanations, the principle has been lately adopted in a few foreign breweries worked on the same lines as the English. To the weight of Jacobsen's authority I owe it that my practical experiments became so soon known in my own land as well as in other countries. Most of them, however, were and are still received by intelligent brewers with distrust. This opposition would have further retarded the adoption of the idea, but for the stout support it has received from Aubry from the very outset. To him belongs the credit of having introduced this reform into Germany. In Bohemia, Belohoubek, and in Norway, Hejberg have made a beginning. Here in Denmark my efforts have been supported by A. Jorgensen and Grunlund. In Jorgensen's laboratory there has been great activity. Not only the numerous breweries in Scandinavia, but most of those in other countries have received their supplies of pure yeast therefrom. In France, Louis Marx has taken up the idea, which but for him would there have scarce borne fruit. Among foreign chemists and botanists who have studied with me, I have found many active co-operators.

The brewery at Old Carlsburg, since the year 1884, and likewise that of New Carlsberg and others, depend entirely on my supplies of pure cultivated yeasts. The fermenting vats at Old Carlsberg contain 9,000 hect. (198,000 galls.) of wort, and the yeast employed in pitching amounts to 2,500 kilogs. (50 cwt.).

Therewith are produced every year 200,000 hect. (122,000 barrels) of lager and export beer. The production at New Carlsberg is very little less. The aggregate value is many millions of marks. The greater part of all this beer is brewed with one species of yeast, that known as Carlsberg bottom-yeast No. 1; the small remaining portion is brewed with another pure cultivated species, that known as Carlsberg bottom-yeast No. 2. I mention these figures to show that we are not dealing with experiments on a small scale, but with solid results in an industry of great magnitude. Glancing at the progress of the reform, we see that it has now found its way into nearly all beer-producing countries. In Denmark and Norway it is now adopted in all the largest breweries. In Sweden a beginning has been made; likewise in Finland, in Bohemia and other parts of the Austrian domains; in Switzerland, North Italy, Belgium, and North America. We find it generally adopted, and established on a solid practical basis in Denmark and Norway, also in Russia, Holland, and Germany, particularly Bavaria. From Old Carlsberg supplies of pure yeast have been sent to breweries in Asia, and from Jorgensen's laboratory to Asia, Australia, and South America. Whether the method has taken root in these remote countries, I am unable to state. What has just been said shows clearly that the system offers certain advantages. Examined more closely, there will be found to be:– 1) That a definite result is assured by determinate means; whereas previously all was problematical. 2) That security is afforded against diseases in beer, which entail serious loss. 3) That a yeast is thus obtained which fetches a higher price in the trade than ordinary impure yeast. 4) That a new development is thus given to industrial production – a consideration of moment to all practical men.

I think I have now sufficiently shown how scientists are step by step working out a great change in our opinions respecting fermentation, and daily adding to our knowledge of its varied properties.

THE PROPERTIES OF STARCH

Starch is a food which is largely required to sustain the human system; it is supplied abundantly in all 'farinaceous' substances (the word merely meaning 'starchy'), such as arrowroot, sago, tapioca, semolina, etc. Arrowroot is prepared from the root stocks of several East and West Indian plants. Sago is also prepared from a deposit in the trunks of several species of palms. Tapioca is got from the roots of the passava tree; but semolina is made from wheat, and, in addition, contains a certain proportion of albuminous gluten; it is therefore more nourishing as a food than any of the above. The three first-named substances are nearly pure starch, when they are unadulterated. But starch is found in one form or other, and in some quantity or other, in nearly all plants. Starch, when seen by the naked eye, is a white, glistening powder, but when viewed through a microscope, it appears like a series of very small semi-transparent grains, of sizes which vary according to the origin of the starch – in some cases they are so minute as the ten-thousandth part of an inch in diameter. The shape of the grain is very irregular, but the different kinds are readily known to a practised eye, the starch from wheat, for example, being different in size and general appearance to that derived from potatoes. Starch is composed of carbon, hydrogen, and oxygen, which enter into its composition always in the same proportions, no matter how the grains may differ in size and appearance. Starch in itself is insoluble, but it is readily changed into a soluble gum called dextrine, and also, by the addition of water, into glucose or sugar. Should anyone wish to extract natural starch from vegetables, let him pound a raw potato in water, and pass it through a fine hair sieve, which will remove the tissue and fibre; then allow the liquid which passes through the sieve to remain until all the starch it carries settles, when the water can be poured off, and pure starch will remain.

DRYNESS OF BREAD MADE FROM ROLLER-GROUND FLOUR

Ever since the introduction of rollers for milling or grinding wheat into flour, the want of moisture in bread has been a vexed question, and not without cause. The upholders of roller-ground flour may rant and rave, and quote statistics to prove their theory that the bread made from it is equally as moist as flour milled in the old system, viz., stone-ground floor. But still the fact remains that, since the introduction of roller-ground flour, bread is drier, has less keeping qualities, and gives a poorer 'yield' per sack than stone-ground flour. So if this is not the cause of the husky dryness in bread noticeable of recent years, what may it be? This may appear to some to be begging the question, but I cannot perceive a better way of sustaining my argument. We are supposed to have better yeast with all the latest chemical improvements – likewise better ovens, with steam generators to ensure moisture, but the dry huskiness still remains. Many a hot argument have I had on this question with men whom one would have thought capable of knowing better. Men who are interested in the manufacture and sale of this particular flour must necessarily put it before the trade in as gilded colours as possible, but say what they will the dryness is still there. I do not for a moment doubt its fine, mellow tint, nor deny that it looks more enticing, and richer to the eye and judgment of purchasers of this commodity, but, as I have said, the dry huskiness remains. For biscuit flour I much prefer it to stone-ground flour, but for batch bread I would not commend it for moisture, general appearance, and yielding powers. I hope no one will accuse me of taking too pessimistic a view of this question, as I believe that the border of it only has been touched. I likewise sincerely believe that there are men capable of overcoming this grave difficulty of the dryness in roller-ground flour – and that in the near future. Now since its cause has been ascertained, and every cause has its corresponding effect, let the effect be removed and the cause will cease. In regard to this question an eminent authority in Paris – M. Lucas, director of the flour market – has recently made a discovery which is of great importance in dealing with it. What, asks M. Lucas, is the cause of roller flour drying out, and being less savoury than burr flour? To this question he gives a plain decisive answer. The baking quality of flour depends chiefly on the oil contained in the germs of the grain. Now, by the roller process, these germs, and along with them the oily matter, are separated from the flour, while they are retained in the burr flour. Hence the better taste and softness of bread made of the latter, which, however, has one defect – the oil retained in it is greatly oxidisable, causing the flour to spoil in a very short time, a circumstance impossible in the former, being devoid of oily matter. Now, as we have found the effect, is there any remedy? M. Lucas says there is. Aimé Girard has found that the quantity of the oil eliminated from the flour by the roller process is 0.21 per cent of the flour's weight. From this knowledge M. Lucas infers that a proper substitute for the oil extracted by this process will give the bread made from roller flour the same baking quality as is possessed by the burr flour. Experiments enabled him to discover that the oil of sweet almonds contains all the qualities necessary to produce the desired result. Almond oil mixed with the dough in the ratio of 2 grammes to 1 kilogramme produced a bread not only just as savoury and elastic as the burr flour bread, but even superior to it, which M. Lucas explains from the fact that the roller flour is not liable to become sour, while the other does after a time. On the other hand, bread made of the same kind of flour without the addition of almond oil invariably proved tasteless and dried out very soon. This experiment was repeated a good many times, and the results submitted to the judgment of experts, who at once and always discovered the difference of the two kinds of bread as to taste and softness, but were at a loss to account for the cause. So the above discovery will be of the greatest importance to all interested in the flour and bread trade.

Thus we have science and art marching side by side (or at least, the little science that we can put to practical use in the baking trade). The abridged extracts from a recent writer on the colour and chemical examination of flour given in a preceding chapter, and the above article on the dryness of roller-ground flour, taken in conjunction with the practical knowledge

I have given in this work, will, I trust, help the breadbaker to more fully understand the varied methods recently adopted in modern flour milling.

THE CAUSES OF HOLES IN BREAD

Why bread should be holey is a question more readily asked than answered. The holes occur in different parts of the loaf, being sometimes between the crumby part and the bottom part of the top crust, and sometimes altogether in the crumby part. In either case the causes are different. One of the primary causes is improper workmanship – such as making the dough, either by hand or machine, in a happy-go-lucky manner; working against time, etc., etc. Scrappy or undermade dough offers less resistance to the accumulated gas, which will follow the track of least resistance more readily than it will follow or force a passage through the better made portion of the dough. Bad moulding is another cause. Let any practical man mould some dough in a soft, flabby manner, and bake a loaf along with his ordinary batch in an oven of extreme heat, and the chances are it will have a hollow, or snuff-box top, and will cut holey all through. I have likewise noticed that a small quantity of bread baked in an oven heated to receive its full complement, with the oven-door open, tends to become holey. Under-proved bread also tends to this result, and should be avoided. Strong yeasts have been erroneously credited with causing holes in bread; I, for one, am inclined to question the truth of this. Weak yeasts cause holes, hut not so strong yeasts. If a piece of dough is made without yeast, and baked in an ordinary oven, a certain quantity of holes will be found. This rather favours the opinion that weak yeasts, and not good strong ones, are to blame for the defect. If this virgin dough is placed in the oven the heat will cause steam to come from it during the process of baking. This steam, when it leaves the dough, leaves a vacancy behind it; if the dough had been properly manipulated, and assisted with healthy fermentation, no holes could occur. Or, to take another instance, viz., home-made bread, when the housewife is short of the staff of life, she will invariably take a part of her sponge dough, mould it round, and pin it out the size of a large plate. She will then place it in the oven without any proof, and the result is heavy, sodden, and holey bread; which at once shows that the defects are due to weakness, as the gluten in this case has not been sufficiently decomposed.

Strong flour is sometimes blamed for causing holes in bread; but my experience contradicts this. In our establishment we are in the habit of using four different grades of flour daily. Our first quality – Hungarian – is a good, strong, rich flour, and bread made from this has no suspicion of the above complaint. Our next in quality is good, strong, double-superfine, and I have never noticed in this any tendency to holey bread. The next we employ is superfine, a strong flour, but darker in colour than either of the above grades: this likewise makes good bread without holes. We have another class, namely fine, weaker in strength and darker in colour than the above. I have sometimes seen bread from this flour inclined to be holey; but never in our strong flours. I may say that this complaint is almost extinct in our establishment.

Potatoes, when used in ferments, if of unsound condition, are likewise to blame for the above defect: for this the remedy at hand is their entire disuse.

But one of the most common causes is the excessive use of low-priced Indian wheat, now used by most millers in the production of cheap flours. This class of wheat is nearly devoid of gluten; and any practical baker knows that the amount of gluten in bread is shown by its rising qualities. The decomposition of gluten facilitates the fermenting qualities of the dough, therefore, no gluten means no rising power. In fermenting, this class of flour has a slow, deadened movement, and feels anything but lively. It also requires a longer time to prove, and when baked has little or no bloom. Extreme beat in the oven is necessary to produce anything approaching bloom on the top. Flour of this grade should be boycotted out of the British market; it is a worry to the journeyman, and a loss to the employer, besides giving but little satisfaction to the public who buy it.

These facts, then, seem to prove that weakness in flour or yeast, or feebleness of fermentative powers under any conditions, are more conducive to holes in bread than when the ingredients used are of a strong and healthy nature.

PERSONAL CLEANLINESS

From a sanitary standpoint, I would suggest that it be made compulsory that all bakers, whether employers, managers, foremen, or journeymen, should undergo a periodical medical examination. There should be no exemption, wherever the parties here referred to are in the habit of manipulating bread, etc. If this proposition were put into force, and carried out as it ought to be, we should only be fulfilling a duty we owe to the public, as well as doing our utmost to prevent the spread of contagious diseases. The details for the above proposal could very simply be arranged for; but as the question at issue is a delicate one, let us for the present draw a veil, with the hope that the idea will only be the germ of a healthier future, both for bakers and our clients, the public. Do not let us be too thin-skinned, and plod on, content to live and work in the old-fashioned style, when we have modern science telling us the penalty we must pay for harbouring the microbes of disease. The necessities of the times demand a change.

On the other hand, we have employers who, as regards exterior appearances, are really too extreme. If they will only modify their ideas as to how a workman should appear at work, the 'masher' baker will soon become a thing of the past. This brings to my mind a story I once heard of a Glasgow employer of this stamp. As the story goes, he advertised for a baker and confectioner. A smart young fellow, who had had the misfortune to be out of work for some time, and whose garments indicated that he was in no way related to the dignified Beau Brumell class, applied for the place. The employer critically eyed the applicant all over, and said, 'Well, my young man, if I offer you the situation, I presume you will be able to come to your work in a better suit of clothes than those you are at present wearing, as I have rather a select trade.' The astonished young man looked at him, and said, 'I beg your pardon, sir; I was not aware that it was a suit of clothes you were advertising for – I thought it was a baker.'

AN APPEAL TO THE TRADE

Unless a desperate effort be at once made to reconstruct the present loose system of making bread, too often carried on in some of our bakeries, the bulk of the bread trade is destined to drift gradually into the hands of female bakers. Members of the trade should not forget that gas and kitchen ovens are getting pretty well perfected, and ovens of this class are cheap and handy. Good yeast can also be had at a low price. Indeed, yeast is at present retailed as ono of our necessary commodities in most provision shops in England. We, likewise, are not ignorant of the fact that the female part of the community has already laid the first plank in that platform which will soon lift them above all forms and customs. Women, in general, are quick in perception, and not very far behind men in reflective powers. Let them once make a passable loaf, and the art of baking becomes so fascinating that they often get baking on the brain. But I have seen bread made by the mother of a large family, that for flavour and colour would vie with that made by many of our so-called professional bread bakers. This is one of those practical facts that so many members of our craft 'pooh-pooh', and try to shirk; but I can assure them that this is one of the leading forces that help to keep the baking trade from gaining that position it is so justly entitled to. It would be for the benefit of the trade to ponder over this, and not forget the old Scotch proverb that 'a steek in time saves nine'.

Another question which appeals very forcibly to everyone connected with the baking trade is that of a representative in Parliament. The mining, agricultural, and other industries are well represented; why, then, should we be exempt from sharing the benefits which are accorded to those whose professions require less skill, and whose responsibility to the masses is neither so far-reaching nor so closely connected with their welfare? If we had a trade representative in Parliament it would open up a new era in our trade, and be another instance of history repealing itself; for did not imperial Borne repeatedly accept and honour one or two of our craft in her dignified Senate?

CONCLUDING REMARKS

Fellow-bakers and workers, do the right and help yourselves; let each one take his part for the advancement of our trade. If this be done as it ought to be done, and the results are not favourable to us as a body of tradesmen, I shall cry 'Peccavi!' and at once humbly submit to correction. But I have confidence that through your energy, courage, and perseverance, a brighter and a better time is looming in the near future for the baking trade.